Vittorio Alfieri

Twayne's World Authors Series
Italian Literature

Anthony Oldcorn, Editor
Brown University

TWAS 732

RITRATTO DI VITTORIO ALFIERI
Painting by Francois-Xavier Fabre,
Palazzo Alfieri, Asti (1798).

Vittorio Alfieri

By Franco Betti
University of California, Los Angeles

Twayne Publishers • Boston

Vittorio Alfieri

Franco Betti

Copyright © 1984 by G. K. Hall & Company
All Rights Reserved
Published by Twayne Publishers
A Division of G. K. Hall & Company
70 Lincoln Street
Boston, Massachusetts 02111

Printed on permanent/durable acid-
free paper and bound in the United
States of America.

Library of Congress Cataloging in Publication Data

Betti, Franco.
  Vittorio Alfieri.

  (Twayne's world authors series ; 732)
  Bibliography: p.
  Includes index.
  1. Alfieri, Vittorio, 1749–1803—Criticism
and interpretation. I. Title. II. Series: Twayne's
world authors series ; TWAS 732.
PQ4682.B4   1984   852'.6   84-582
ISBN 0-8057-6579-4

Contents

About the Author

Franco Betti, a native of Florence, Italy, is Professor of Italian at the University of California, Los Angeles, where he has been teaching since 1965. He holds a Ph.D. in Romance Languages and Literatures, and Romance Philology, from the University of California, Berkeley.

Mr. Betti's main field of specialization is Italian Literature of the eighteenth century. His publications, however, include essays on authors such as Petrarch, Boccaccio, Ariosto, Foscolo, and Croce. Mr. Betti is also the author of books of poetry and fiction.

Preface

By projecting all the passionate complexity of his personality upon the stage, Vittorio Alfieri gave Italy a tragic theater that had both the elegance of line of a neoclassical structure and the boldness and despair of a Romantic heart. The world of Greek tragedy, with its sense of implacable destiny, filtered through the Roman writers and the experience of the Italian tradition, was brought to react with the sociopolitical reality of the second half of the eighteenth century in a unique creative synthesis.

Throughout the nineteenth century, however, Alfieri was admired and revered mainly because of the libertarian ideals animating his tragic production. The myth of an Alfieri constantly engaged in a heroic struggle against tyranny endured until recent times. But, nowadays, rather than looking in awe at Alfieri the man, we prefer to savor his poetry.

The man envisioned by the patriotic critics of the Romantic era was a rather monochromatic figure characterized mainly by his love for freedom and his wish for an independent, unified Italy. But although this aspect of Alfieri's personality is undeniable, the poet himself is a much more intriguing and disquieting character.

Alfieri was the author of a great variety of works in different genres, but it is his tragic theater and his autobiography that excel over all others. Accordingly, the main thrust of this essay has been to place them in sharper focus, fitting them into the context of the "minor" works that gravitate around them. In so doing, I have made a particular effort to furnish—along with critical analysis—enough factual information to render this presentation more accessible to the reader unfamiliar with Alfieri's works. Furthermore, since the last phase of his creative activity shifted toward the comic theater, that too is analyzed here and placed in its proper perspective.

I have attempted to capture the essence of Alfieri's personality in its main characteristics: the provincial aristocrat turned cosmopolitan "philosophe," on the one hand, and the creator of enduring tragic characters on the other. To achieve this goal I have made ample use of both the work and the many commentaries he kept addressing to posterity. I have attempted, in other words, to reconstruct his poetic world from within, by reconciling the various "messages" he left and at the same time relating them to the background of the cultural and the historical realities of his times. For this purpose, while relying constantly on the texts, I have kept external references to the essential.

At this point I would like to take the opportunity to express my gratitude to my colleagues Giovanni Cecchetti and Fredi Chiappelli for their support and advice during the preparation of this book.

Franco Betti

University of California, Los Angeles

Chronology

1749   Vittorio Alfieri, son of Count Antonio Amedeo Alfieri di Cortemilia and Monica Maillard di Tournon, born in Asti, Piedmont, on January 16.

1758   Attends the Royal Academy, in Turin.

1766   Graduates from the Academy. As an ensign in the Royal Army is assigned to the Provincial Regiment in Asti. Begins his restless travels with journeys to Milan, Florence, and Rome.

1767   Travels to Genoa, Marseilles, and Paris.

1768   Is introduced to Louis XV, at Versailles. Journey to London, then to Holland, where he experiences his first intoppo amoroso ("amorous encounter").

1769   In Turin, reads from the French "philosophes" and Rousseau. First enthusiasm for Plutarch's Lives.

1770   After traveling in Austria and Germany, goes to Denmark, Sweden, and Russia.

1771   Second passionate love affair with Penelope Pitt, the first wife of Earl Ligonier of Clonmell, in London.

1772   Returns to Turin after traveling in France, Spain, and Portugal.

1774   Love affair with the wife of the Marquis Turinetti di Priè. First draft of Cleopatra, successfully performed the following year.

1775   Decides to dedicate himself to the writing of tragedies. Conceives Filippo and Polinice.

1776   Travels to Tuscany. Conceives Antigone, Agamennone, Oreste, Don Garzia. Returns to Turin.

1777   Second voyage to Tuscany; first idea of Virginia;
        establishes a close friendship with Francesco Gori-
        Gandellini, in Siena. There he conceives the Con-
        giura de' Pazzi (The Conspiracy of the Pazzi),
        writes On Tyranny; writes in prose Agamennone,
        Oreste, Virginia. In October, goes to Florence
        where he meets his degno amore ("the woman worthy
        of his love"), Luisa Stolberg, Countess of Albany,
        wife of Charles Edward Stuart, pretender to the
        English Throne.

1778   Abandons Piedmont for good, freeing himself from
        any military obligation and ceding his lands and
        properties to his sister. In Florence studies the
        classical authors. Works intensely on his trage-
        dies; writes the poem Etruria vendicata (Etruria
        avenged) and the ode All'America Libera (To free
        America).

1783   His first ten tragedies printed in Siena. Travels
        across Italy, then to France and England.

1784   Back in Italy, then in Alsace, where he conceives
        Agide, Sofonisba, and Mirra. Death of his
        "incomparable" friend Gori-Gandellini.

1785   Writes the Panegirico di Plinio a Traiano (Pliny
        panegiric to Trajan) and works on Del Principe e
        delle Lettere (The Prince and Letters).

1786   Completes Del Principe e delle Lettere, drafts
        La Virtù sconosciuta (Unacknowledged virtue);
        conceives and partially puts into verse the "trame-
        logedy" Abele, drafts Bruto I (The First
        Brutus) and Bruto II (The Second Brutus) and
        works at his theater in general. Writes also his
        first Satire; composes many sonnets. Travels
        with the Countess; they take up residence in Paris
        the following year.

1789   First outbreaks of the French Revolution welcomed
        with an ode by Alfieri. Editions of his works at
        Kehl and Paris.

1790   Translations from the classics; writes his autobi-
        ography.

1792   Escapes from the excesses of Jacobin Paris and establishes himself in Florence. Writes many poems and two Satire.

1794   Acts in the title roles in Saul, Bruto I, and Filippo.

1795   Steps up his study of the classics; more translations. Works on the Misogallo (The hater of the French).

1796   Composes more Satire and studies Greek.

1798   Completes the Misogallo; revises his Rime (Poems) and Vita.

1800   Conceives his Commedie (Comedies).

1801   The comedies are written in prose; then the first four are put into verse. In September he falls ill.

1802   Works on the comedies and translates Aristophanes. New illness.

1803   Continues to work on his Vita; refines the verse of the comedies. Dies in Florence on October 8 in the arms of his beloved Countess.

Chapter One
The Birth of a Theater

The Author

Vittorio Alfieri was born on the eve of the second half of the eighteenth century, on January 17, 1749. A year earlier an important historical event had taken place in Europe: the Peace of Aix-la-Chapelle, which brought to an end the Austrian wars of succession—a power struggle which had engaged all major European states.

The political structure determined by that event enjoyed a certain stability and lasted for about four decades, until the crisis of 1789 and the French Revolution (1). That span of time encompassed most of Alfieri's life (he died in 1803) and saw the major body of his work—his tragic theater—come into existence.

Alfieri is commonly regarded as one of the greatest Italian poets, yet in his lifetime Italy did not yet exist as a political entity. It had a geographical unity and a religious one as well, but even culturally—given the heterogeneous composition of its many dialects—the matter of oneness remained dubious. Alfieri was born in Piedmont and was therefore a citizen of the Kingdom of Sardinia. Only later did he make the laborious and successful attempt to, as he put it, "de-piedmontize" himself. Such an enterprise required him not only to surrender his commission in the Royal Guard and to give up the bulk of his estate, but also to master the Italian language as it was spoken in Tuscany, for his first language, if we exclude the Piedmontese dialect, had actually been French.

The Italy of Alfieri's time was indeed a jigsaw puzzle of states, many of which were independent in theory only. Piedmont, however, was independent and, under the centuries-old rule of the House of Savoy, had been able in the early eighteenth century to extend its territory to include the island of Sardinia, from which the Kingdom now took its name. However, with the peace of Aix-la-Chapelle, the Savoyard expansionistic policy came to an end. This was due to several reasons, but mainly to the

1

fact that Lombardy, on Piedmont's eastern border, was now under the direct control of Austria and was practically impregnable, as was the territory of Genoa, to the South, under the protection of France. At the same time, King Charles Emmanuel III's sincere desire for peace—after twenty years of war—should be taken into consideration as a more than legitimate reason.

At the date of Alfieri's birth, then, Piedmont was in a stage of consolidation. This was for the Kingdom of Sardinia an historical era characterized by an almost xenophobic sense of closedness to any outside influence, backed by a stubborn determination to preserve the old absolutist (feudal) structure of the state (2). In neighboring Lombardy the Austrian regime that had come to power after almost two centuries of stifling Spanish domination was about to promote—under the aegis of enlightened despotism—a climate of social and economic changes and progress. Piedmont, on the other hand, was to experience a rather high degree of sociopolitical involution.

Charles Emmanuel III devoted all his energy to the Kingdom's internal administration, on which he reserved to himself all power of decision. Even the public—and all too often the private—lives of his subjects were directly regulated by the monarch's sense of austere morality. So much so that in an epoch in which most European courts were marked by a careless spirit of gaiety and luxury, the capital of the kingdom of Sardinia, Turin, offered to the outsider a drab picture of stiff social rules and behavior (3). Bearing this in mind, we can better understand why the young and impetuous Alfieri decided to relinquish his position in such a society.

In his autobiography Alfieri has left us both a most intimate account of his public and private life and a vivid picture of the Italy—indeed of most of Europe—of his time. We shall see, however, that his role on the political scene was mainly that of a brooding, pessimistic observer. Only when forced by unavoidable circumstances will he become a participant of a sort in contemporary historical events—witness his dramatic escape from Paris during the revolutionary movements of 1792-93 (4). Yet we would be hard put to find another poet of his time who had a stronger sense of history than Vittorio Alfieri.

The fact is that he was never willing, nor able, to

lower his lofty, aristocratic, heroic ideals and libertarian aspirations to the level of the political reality
of the Italian states in the second half of the eighteenth century. All the inner strength of his passionate
character, inspired and nurtured by the examples of the
great heroes of antiquity as he had come to know them
through the pages of Plutarch, could only find a proper
mode of expression in love and poetry.

The constantly felt antagonistic discrepancy between
the heroic humanity he dreamed of and the present-day
reality determined the ideological and emotional tension
that will become typical of the Romantic idealists of the
turn of the century, and which we find in both Alfieri
the man and Alfieri the poet.

Looking around at what he regarded as a dismal, hopeless political situation, he could not recognize among
his contemporaries any of the larger-than-life heroes he
felt were needed to establish the new order of things
envisioned by the philosophy of the Enlightenment. Only
through the creation of tragic characters, capable of
<u>feeling</u> at the highest level of human emotion, could
Alfieri find a way to channel the dictates of a strong,
individualistic will, and to transform them into symbolic
action.

A Tragic Vocation

Alfieri wrote his first tragic composition, <u>Antonio e
Cleopatra</u> (<u>Antony and Cleopatra</u>), in 1774, at the age
of twenty-five. A year later, following the first per-
formance of that work, his literary "conversion" had,
according to the <u>Vita</u> (his autobiography), taken place:
he had become certain of his vocation as a writer of
tragedies (5). By that time he had already traveled
widely throughout Europe: from Paris, where he had been
introduced to Louis XV, to England, from Spain to Russia
and Sweden. He had also experienced three tumultuous
love affairs: in Holland, England, and Italy.

It was in Turin, during a period of convalescence of
his current flame, the wife of the Marquis Turinetti di
Priè, that he attempted to write his first tragedy. The
subject matter was inspired by chance, it seems, by a
tapestry in the lady's palazzo, where episodes from the
love story of Antony and Cleopatra were represented (6).
The surface account of the incident conceals of course

certain determining factors other than those dictated by
mere chance. Alfieri had been, and still was, at that
time, trying his hand at poetry. The verses he later
rejected bear the stamp of the then fashionable "Arcadian," pastoral poetry, and many of those compositions seem
metrically, rhythmically, and stylistically close to the
verses of Pietro Metastasio (1698-1782), the most illustrious Italian poet of the time (7). Later, under the
pretext of patriotism, Alfieri displayed disdain, and
even contempt, for his famous colleague; but we should
not exclude another, and more compelling reason for his
hostility—rivalry (8). We might thus assume that the
aspiring young poet was emulating the acclaimed
Metastasio, and not simply following the example of the
French poets of the preceding century, such as Corneille
and Racine, as he himself declared.

As a matter of fact, Metastasio had already done just
that, and he had chosen to project his poetical creations
against the background of classical antiquity. It is
true that Alfieri, in writing his tragedies, was influ-
enced by the reading of Plutarch, and by the study of
Italian authors such as Dante and Machiavelli, but it
would be wrong to exclude the more immediate example of a
poet whose contemporary fame was as great as Metastasio's
—perhaps not just as an example to be imitated, but
rather as one to be surpassed.

The two poets had in fact completely different tempera-
ments. In Metastasio's melodramma, a grandiose opera
where poetry, music, and pomp were uniquely harmonized,
the emphasis is on the musicality of the language needed
to express the sentimentality of the characters. Where
Metastasio was sentimental and superficial, Alfieri was
willful and profound; where the language of the first
tended to become music, the other's stylistic mode will
resort to harshness and vigorously hammered out rhythmic
phrases. Furthermore, while Metastasio was a consummate
courtier who wrote during most of his career under the
patronage of the Austrian emperor, Alfieri was fiercely
independent.

In any event, well before Alfieri's "conversion," the
fashionable Arcadian poetry that had culminated in
Metastasio's synthesis of poetry and music had run its
course. Both public and critics alike had proclaimed
their rebellion—as was well illustrated by Saverio
Bettinelli (1718-1808) in his Virgilian Letters (1758)—
under the banner of a poetics that clamored for "things,

not words," thus implying a renewal not only in content but in style (9). Alfieri responded above and beyond the cultural imperative of his time.

An important factor contributing toward the choice of the tragic form must be identified with Alfieri's aspiration toward the highest level of poetical achievement, the level which tradition assigned to tragedy. This aspiration remained dominant even though he never gave up writing lyric poetry, mostly in the canonized form of the sonnet (10). As for the fortuitous first spark of inspiration—the love story of Antony and Cleopatra, Alfieri himself reminds us of his own identification with Antony, enslaved by love, as he saw himself falling under the embarrassing spell of the Marchioness Turinetti di Prié (11).

That Alfieri's first theatrical labor was not very successful, that it was rejected by the author himself as a failure, does not really matter. What is significant is the fact that it marked, historically, the birth of Italy's modern tragic theater. True, tragedy had begun to flourish in Italy during the Age of the Renaissance. Giangiorgio Trissino (1478-1550), deriving his inspiration from the classical works of Sophocles and Euripides, composed the first Italian tragedy, Sofonisba, between 1514 and 1515. Other authors, such as Giovanni Rucellai (1475-1525), Giambattista Giraldi Cintio (1504-1573), and Pietro Aretino (1492-1556) were also hard at work. Even an already famous poet like Torquato Tasso (1544-1595) met the challenge of the tragic theater with his Torrismondo (1586) (12).

The following century, the Age of the Baroque, saw the successful growth and expansion of the melodramma, or opera, born out of, as we mentioned above, the felicitous union of drama and music. Yet, tragedy held its own with works by Federico Della Valle (1560-1628) and Carlo De' Dottori (1618-1685). In Alfieri's own century at least one author, Scipione Maffei (1675-1755), had acquired an international reputation with his Merope (1713), a tragedy that was even going to be imitated in France by the celebrated Voltaire (1694-1778).

In spite of all this activity, the Italian tragic theater could not boast authors such as Shakespeare (1564-1616), the Spanish Lope De Vega (1562-1635) and Calderón de la Barca (1600-1681), the French Pierre Corneille (1606-1684) and Louis Racine (1692-1763). Not until Alfieri.

The First Tragedies

From the very beginning of his career as a tragic poet, Alfieri adopted a working method which he never abandoned (13). It consisted of three phases (respiri —"breaths"), or stages of composition, which he broke down as follows: first, the conception (ideare) of the tragedy; second, the act of writing down (stendere) a prose draft in five acts; and third, the versification (versificare) of the composition. The conception involved the writing of a few pages (at times just one page) consisting of the names of the characters and the distribution, act by act, of the scenes and their content. The sketching out of the five acts made up the second phase, and it was done very rapidly, approximately one act per day, with no concern for style—mainly in prose, but with the intrusion of "bad" lines of poetry as well. What counted most during this stage was the "strong feeling," the passion, which he had to experience himself and which had to be put down on paper in the most urgent manner possible. Alfieri felt that if he were not successful in doing this, he could not produce a good tragedy. The final stage was then achieved by selecting "the best thoughts" and transposing them into verse.

Alfieri was convinced that once the work reached the third stage successfully, the stylistic concern—now necessary—could not hurt or impede the immediate expression of powerful feelings which he regarded as the preeminent quality of a good tragedy. In fact, this preoccupation with the immediacy of the feelings, which had to be kept alive at all costs within the structure of the work in its total unfolding, remains possibly the most relevant characteristic of Alfieri's theater, and forms the very foundation of his poetics.

Filippo

After the rejected Antony and Cleopatra, Alfieri's first acknowledged tragedy, the Filippo (Philip) is one of his best. Though first conceived in 1775, it was not published until 1783, after intensive revision—from the first draft in French prose, on down. The revision went well beyond even the edition of 1783, for Alfieri kept polishing his Philip to the last minute, before the Paris printing of his works in 1790 (14).

The final Philip should therefore be regarded as a work of the poet's maturity, not of his apprenticeship. In fact, the unity, the organic quality of style, that characterizes Alfieri's best works—and for that matter his entire theater—stems precisely from this constant care in revising and refining them, down through the years. In a way, the poet, in certain periods of intense labor, worked on all of his tragedies at the same time. Such a situation makes it somewhat arbitrary, a mere question of practicality, to analyze them in a given chronological sequence.

Only later, in his treatise Del Principe e delle Lettere (The Prince and Letters), will Alfieri dwell at length on the work and function of the poet as seen in his relationship to society and the state. Many of the principles expounded in the Prince clarify and justify the tragedies he had already written, and those still to come. One such principle remains at the basis of all of Alfieri's works; it is the supremacy given to historical events as a source of inspiration. Not a novelty in itself, it is noteworthy because of the extreme faith Alfieri had in it: "The author succeeds in arousing emotions in many ways; but in no way more effectively than by depicting in noble, moving, and strong colors, enterprises great in themselves from which important results have sprung. He generally achieves this by poetic fiction, or by drawing on historical sources . . ." (15). Philip provides the first successful implementation of this basic principle.

The action takes place in Madrid around the year 1568. It centers around the figures of the Hapsburg Emperor Philip II (1527-1598)—whose name gives the play its title—his son by a former marriage, Don Carlos, and Isabella, his queen. The drama is precipitated by the jealousy aroused in the emperor by his suspicion of a love affair between Don Carlos and Isabella. The jealousy is masked under a trumped-up accusation of treason. Only two secondary characters enrich the plot, introducing the elements (complementary to the main protagonists) of generous friendship—Perez—on the one hand, and the most abject, villainous kind of courtiership—Gomez—on the other. The tension of the situation culminates with the death of both Isabella and Don Carlos.

Alfieri has the action adroitly begin with a soliloquy

spoken by Isabella. By introducing the only feminine
presence in the drama before any other, the author establishes an aura of frail beauty, an aura reinforced in the
form of her name, Isabella, which Alfieri substituted for
the alternative form, Elisabetta. Her soliloquy presents
her secret: love in all the complexity of its contrasting elements. Through her words we also get a glimpse of
the young hero before he appears on the scene. Isabella's doubts, fears, the hopelessness of the situation are
all concentrated in her rhetorical question: "Philip's
faithless wife / Dare I behold with fondness Philip's
son?" There the menacing repetition of the emperor's
name, with its double possessive, establishes forthwith a
sense of tyrannical ownership. But her love seems to be
determined by a superior force: "Yet who beholds that
son and loves him not?"; for Don Carlos is endowed with:

> A heart though bold, humane; a lofty nature;
> An intellect sublime; and in a form
> Most fair, a soul of corresponding worth.
>
> [1.1]

With the rhetorical question on her lips, Isabella suc-
cumbs to a passion stronger than her will.

Her preoccupation will henceforth be to keep her feeling hidden from the world, with the sad awareness, however, that even though she may succeed in deceiving
others, she cannot deceive herself—a situation that
seems to anticipate the inner conflict of a later tragedy, Mirra (Myrrha).

Alfieri's first heroine foreshadows the Romantic
conflict between heart and reason—with the balance tip-
ping in favor of the heart. She reminds one of Dante's
Francesca da Rimini. We know from his Vita that
Alfieri was an avid reader of Dante's Divine Comedy,
and surely he must have been greatly fascinated by the
tragic account of Francesca's passion for her brother-in-
law, Paolo. Thus in the second scene, when Don Carlos
appears and is troubled by the fact that Isabella wants
to avoid him, she reassures him, weaving into her speech
an allusion to her native land: "Quel dolce primo / Amor
del suol natio" ("That sweet, first love for one's native
soil"). The motif as well as the rhythm and cadence of
the phrase remind us of Francesca and her nostalgic
description of her place of origin.

Don Carlos, we are told, is handsome, noble, and generous of heart; he possesses all the basic qualities of a heroic character. However, he does not really succeed in achieving a truly tragic dimension, except perhaps in the final death scene. As the "good" character destined to be crushed by the "evil" one, he is overshadowed by Isabella. It is she who, an innocent caught in the middle of father-son oedipal rivalry—she had been promised to Carlos until Philip changed his mind and married her himself—assumes the full role of victim, thereby depriving the character of the young prince of a greater share of our sympathy. Again, how can we forget Dante's Paolo, upstaged by Francesca, silently weeping at her side as she emotionally relates their tragic story.

Alfieri titled his tragedy <u>Philip</u> rather than <u>Don Carlos</u>, contrary to the practice of several later European poets who treated the same subject. Philip is clearly the character who gripped Alfieri's imagination most, in his multiple role as tyrant, pitiless father, and cruel husband. The moving force of the tragedy is hate rather than love. Love is only the catalyst which serves to precipitate the action.

Philip, according to a recurring technique, does not appear until the second act, but we already know him through Don Carlos and Isabella. His invisible presence has already permeated the stage with a funereal gloom and hopelessness that his physical appearance can only accentuate. The resulting atmosphere of ineluctability weighs on the entire action and lends to it that oppressive quality that the poet wanted to achieve. From Don Carlos we had learned about Philip's hatred of him, "Suddito e figlio / Di assoluto signor" ("at once subject, and son, of monarch absolute" [1.2]), and about "gli avvolgimenti infami / D'empia corte" ("treacherous intrigues of this vile court"). The theme of intrigue is strengthened by the words of Isabella, who, in order to alleviate Carlos's pain, suggests that in the emperor's heart there could be no hate, only the suspicions of betrayal planted there by his base courtiers.

Philip's way of ascertaining Isabella's love for his son is devious. He accentuates the element of political betrayal and is aided in this by his minister, Gomez. Don Carlos is accused of plotting against the throne by supporting the cause of the rebellious Netherlands. All this is artfully done, in such a way that Isabella cannot help betraying herself. As Philip already knew her feelings—as well as his own—toward Don Carlos, he finds

in the plot a way to justify his own behavior, not merely
to the others, but to himself.

Only in the fifth scene of the fourth act are we told
by Gomez, who has penetrated the heart and mind of his
lord, the reason for Philip's hate: envy. Gomez reveals
the truth to the queen in the process of lying to her in
order to bring her feelings out into the open: "in veder
virtù verace / Tanta nel figlio, la virtù mentita / Del
rio padre si adira" ("Philip's simulated virtue / Cannot
endure the painful spectacle / Of undissembled virtue in
a son"). He then adds, speaking of the emperor, "ed,
empio, ei vuole / Pria spento il figlio, che di sè mag-
giore" ("Impious in his envy, he prefers / To that superiority, his death"). Intuitively, we knew this all along.
In fact, ever since the confrontation of the second act,
the fate of the two victims has been taking shape in
Philip's mind. Don Carlos has also fully understood,
and, at the beginning of the third act, he communicates
his fear to Isabella, begging her, for her own sake,
never to pronounce his name with pity to the emperor, for
"Grave oltraggio al tiranno è un cor pietoso" ("The
spectacle of pity in another / Maddens the cruel bosom of
a tyrant").

In the following scenes Philip accuses his son before
the Council of State, stating that he has tried to murder
him. Gomez adds that Don Carlos is also conspiring with
France; therefore, he should be put to death. After a
stormy confrontation between father and son, ending with
the arrest of Don Carlos, the fourth act centers mainly
on Isabella. She is told by Philip of Don Carlos's impri-
sonment, and afterwards is informed by Gomez of the death
sentence decreed by the Council upon the prince. Gomez,
feigning pity and understanding, offers to arrange a meeting between the two of them. In the final act, the first
scene has Don Carlos alone, meditating on his destiny—
fearing death, but at the same time welcoming it. His
greatest concern is for his beloved Isabella. He fears
for her safety, he fears that Philip has discovered his
love for the queen and that he will take revenge upon
her, "Che del tiranno la vendetta sempre / Suol prevenir
l'offesa" ("Vengeance that always, where a tyrant rules /
Precedes the crime").

Don Carlos finally realizes that Isabella has been
betrayed by the devious courtier Gomez, but nothing can
be done, for at that moment Philip appears upon the
scene. Philip's first words echo Don Carlos's: "tutta

or m'è d'uopo / La mia virtude; or, che fatal si appres-
sa / L'ora di morte . . ." ("I have need to summon all my
fortitude / Now that the fatal hour of death approaches"), confirming them and adding to them the ring of
unescapable doom: "Ora di morte è giunta: / Perfido, è
giunta: io te l'arreco" ("Perfidious one, that hour of
death is come: I bring it to thee"). Isabella realizes
with horror that they have indeed been betrayed. Don
Carlos declares his readiness for death, but the emperor
wants first to abuse them verbally. It is now that they
are really bound together as one couple. Philip's hatred
actually joins them forever:

> Wretch, thou shalt die: but first, ye impious pair,
> My fulminating accents hear, and tremble.
> Ye vile ones! long, yes, long I've known it all.
> That horrid flame that burns in you with love.
> In me with fury, long has fix'd its torment.

After the emperor has threatened them with his vengeance, a "revenge full, unexampled," we are led to
believe that his fury is not really aroused by jealousy—
for he could never have loved anyone like Isabella—but
by the offense done to him, to his pride, as king. In
his words: "Thou hast in me the king offended, then /
And not thy lover!" However, his impassioned words are
indeed dictated by jealousy, and, again, he is only trying to avoid admitting the origin of his feelings so as
not to suffer any further humiliation. This remains true
even if we regard him as an exclusively political man, a
tyrant embodying a state that imposes the ironclad laws
of its necessities upon him.

It is indeed Philip who acquires the accents of a
tragic character. He becomes a man capable of experien-
cing the force of hatred so strongly as to crave for the
blood of his own son and of his wife. The action culminates with the offering of a dagger and a cup of poison
to the two innocent victims. Don Carlos stabs himself
with the blade presented to him by the evil Gomez—the
same blade which the latter has just used to murder
Carlos's trusted friend Perez. Isabella is ready to take
the poison, but Philip now wants to make his revenge even
more cruel by denying it to her:

> Thou shalt live
> Spite of thyself, shalt live . . .

Yes, thou
Sever'd from him, shalt live; live days of woe;
Thy ling'ring grief will be a joy to me.
And when at last, recover'd from thy love,
Thou wishest to live on, I, then, will kill thee.

But Isabella grabs the dagger and kills herself, thus
leaving Philip alone, his vengeance accomplished, but
with a bitter question on his lips: "I have at last
obtain'd an ample, and horrid vengeance . . . But am I
happy?" These words reveal his feelings directly for the
first time, and make us better understand his existential
drama, torn between conflicting impulses of a father, a
husband, and a tyrant.

The Awareness of Poetics

The most relevant structural elements of Philip
break down, following Alfieri's own suggestion, into (a)
invention; (b) arrangement of scenes (sceneggiatura);
(c) style. The three components correspond roughly to
the three stages of Alfieri's method of composition, and
an analysis of them may help to determine and understand
Alfieri's poetics. In the first tragedy all the aesthetic principles of Alfieri's theater are already well
established; they will remain constant in all his works,
in spite of the diversification of situation and characters. He said of his body of work that if it had a
fault, it would be the one of uniformity, to the point
that if one were to examine and understand the structure
(ossatura) of any one of his tragedies, one would understand all of them. We might disagree with Alfieri in
judging such organic uniformity as a defect, but we can
certainly accept the rest of his statement as realistic
and helpful (16).
    If we consider the central element of structure, the
arrangement of scenes or sceneggiatura, we can easily
discern in Philip the characteristics of Alfieri's
general scheme. They are: a brief first act; the appearance of the protagonist by the second act; a lack of
incidents compensated for by dialogue; the fifth act as
brief and "rushing" as possible, with the emphasis on
action; the speeches of the dying hero being kept to a
minimum. The norm of the Aristotelian unities (time,
place, and action) was faithfully espoused by the author,

but the unity that he considered really important was that of action. According to him, when one narrates, or shows, a certain event, the listener, or spectator, does not wish to hear or see anything else that might distract him or lessen his concentration.

Even if we do not choose to regard the primacy of the unity of action as an Alfierian anticipation of Romantic aesthetics, it is nevertheless easy to see how well it suited his passionate nature. A natural inclination led him toward that spiritual and aesthetic principle of the forte sentire ("strong feeling"), which he sought in his characters—as he did in himself—and led in turn to the artistic necessity of a continuous rushing, and unity, of the tragic action. This characteristic typifies Alfieri's work. The subjective dimension of his spiritual biography is injected into the sphere of the historical characters that populate his theater.

In the second printing of his tragedies (1789) Alfieri methodically stated his "opinions" on them. But he had already attempted to clarify the nature of his work by answering two critical letters written to him in 1783 and 1785 respectively, by noted men of letters: Ranieri De' Calsabigi (1714-1795), and the better-known Melchiorre Cesarotti (1730-1808). In his reply to Calsabigi, Alfieri stated that he had tried to give form to a tragedy that would meet the following prerequisites: five acts, all of them as filled as possible with one single subject, woven on one main thread only; the drama of the situation expressed by the main characters without the aid of confidants or spectators, as rapidly as the passion (which nevertheless requires a certain amount of time to unfold) would allow it; as simply as possible; as gloomy and ferocious as nature can be; and, above all, as passionate as he felt within (17).

Although the letter is more lively, animated as it is by an immediate thrust of polemical enthusiasm in explaining the originality of his work to his correspondent, the statement is very close to his later, more pondered and articulate "opinion."

In this subdivision of tragical prerequisites, the defense of soliloquy is very significant. To his correspondent's contention that the frequency of such a technique is boring and not verisimilar, he answered that a soliloquy, when it is not too long, and when it reflects the passionate character of a great hero, is much to be preferred to a dialogue of the same content with a confi-

dant. The mere presence of a character who is not moved
by the same feeling as the main protagonist would only
tend to dampen the scene and alienate the participation
of the audience. As for the possible lack of verisimilitude induced by such a device, Alfieri dismissed it by
bringing as proof of the legitimacy of soliloquy the fact
that he himself indulged quite often in such a mode of
self-expression—another revealing example of how much
the poet identified emotionally with the characters he
was creating.

In the particular case of Philip the author points
out that the play begins with a soliloquy of Isabella's.
She unfolds her inner conflict between love and duty
directly, and not through a confidant, as had been the
case in a first draft of the tragedy. Such a noble
character could not reveal her innermost feelings to a
social and spiritual inferior. Alfieri insists on this
mode of expression with a profusion of examples. For
him, all extremes of passion tend to concentrate in man's
heart, rather than becoming externalized in conversation.
Only weak souls—and feelings—find solace in words,
thus becoming, at most, tender, but not tragic personages.

Concerning the notion of invention, Alfieri makes a
sharp distinction: if by invention we understand the
treatment of a subject that has never been treated before, he felt that no one had "invented" less than he
had. If, on the other hand, we give the word a wider
meaning, that of creating something new out of a well-
known subject—as was the case with all the Greek and
Roman subject matter he made his—then he was certain no
other author had created more. He has his originality
reside mainly in the method he employed in dealing with
any given subject. It goes without saying that the line
of separation between the method in question and the
arrangement of scenes is somewhat tenuous. In speaking
of his method Alfieri has in mind the treatment of the
plot, the line of action, and its unfolding on the stage.
It has to do with the number of characters, who will be
reduced to four, and above all with the treatment of peri-
pheral incidents, which will be completely eliminated.
Such a principle of elimination coincides in essence with
Alfieri's defense of the soliloquy.

The new structure of tragedy Alfieri felt he had
identified tended therefore toward a maximum of concentration of the essential elements. All the spurious

mechanisms—and props—traditionally used on the stage, such as ghosts, lightning and thunder, eavesdropping on confidential conversations, useless killing, nonverisimilar recognitions, secret notes, locks of hair, and similar devices he called mezzucci or "cheap means." These are absent from his theater. The dynamics of the action are supplied by the simple and natural means suggested by the situation itself. The author followed with particular care two main expedients: never to have the subject of the drama introduced in the first act by an ad hoc character created merely for that purpose; and never to substitute in the final act a narrative for what could be seen on the stage without offending common decency and verisimilitude. Should it be absolutely necessary, the narrative had to be delivered, not by a messenger—as it was traditionally done—but by one of the main protagonists.

In stressing the originality of his theater, Alfieri was ready to challenge the critic to a comparison between his works and those of other Italian and French authors such as Scipione Maffei (1675-1755), Crebillon (1674-1762), and Voltaire (1694-1788). He does not mention directly the English theater, or Shakespeare, as Calsabigi himself praised Shakespeare's originality, and the fact that he had chosen to represent nature in all its raw force, without embellishments. Calsabigi also approved of the use of all the devices and props which were, on the contrary, condemned by Alfieri; he only deplored the fact that the English author had employed such devices ad nauseam (18).

We may surmise that when Alfieri stresses the originality he had achieved without the support of what he considered mezzucci, or cheap means, he was so doing because he was moved by a polemical attitude toward the work of the famous British playwright and his followers.

Both Alfieri's and Calsabigi's statements were dictated by the rationalistic aesthetics which had been evolving in Italy for almost a century as a consequence of the anti-baroque reaction typified by the Academy of the Arcadia and exemplified in the works of Gianvincenzo Gravina (1664-1718) and Ludovico Muratori (1672-1750)—to mention only two of the most influential theoreticians of that time. The same aesthetics were at the basis of the neoclassical literary theory and practice which dominated the second half of the eighteenth century (19).

Neoclassical principles will also be evident in

Alfieri's view of his stylistic originality. He was
convinced, as he wrote to both Calsabigi and Cesarotti,
that he had forged a personal style. It was unique in
its brevity, simplicity, dignity, and energy; it was
fully worthy of the definition of tragic. He does
admit to certain defects, especially in the early period
of his activity; he recognizes that his style is somewhat
obscure and harsh, though boasting that the same imputa-
tion had been brought against Dante's Divine Comedy.
He admits to having made an overabundant use of preposi-
tions and monosyllables which tended to give his verses a
choppy, tormented rhythm, but he is quick to add that he
had done so in order to avoid the singsong trivialities
that, he felt, were emasculating the Italian poetry of
his time (20).

A Political Consciousness

In other speculative works Alfieri places the issue of
poetry, politics, and morality in tight correlation.
Essays such as the Prince and Letters (1789) and On
Tyranny (1789) bring to the fore two most cogent issues:
on the one hand, they make a contribution to the traditional debate on the purpose of literature and the function of the writer in society; on the other hand, they
delineate a sharper profile of the figure of the tyrant
(21). While the common denominator of both works is the
figure of the prince, what connects them is in fact the
author's desire to define a personal line of poetics. In
The Prince and Letters a particular theme recurring
with regular frequency is the debate about the "usefulness" and "delectability" of literature. The third
chapter of the first book of the Prince defines the
theme: Alfieri seems to accept fully the Horatian principle of miscere utile dulci ("mixing the useful and the
pleasurable"). At the time, the principle of combining
instruction with textual pleasure had already been well
integrated with the philosophy of the Enlightenment,
which, however, stressed the utilitarian component of the
classical principle.

Alfieri's brief chapter condenses many of the issues
current in his age—the age, we may remember, of "enlightened despotism"—and can be regarded as typical of the
polemical interrelation Alfieri establishes among letters, politics, and morality. If letters are intended to

instruct by developing the heart of man, "inducing toward good, dissuading him from evil, enlarging his ideas, filling him with noble and useful enthusiasm," they cannot, however, achieve these goals under the auspices of a monarchical form of government (22).

From this perspective, even literary style is determined—and regulated—by the absolutist regime. According to Alfieri: "The predominating characteristics of a work of genius originating in a principality must then necessarily be rather elegance of expression than sublimity and force of thought." Princes in general, in their policy of subjugating letters, have deflected them more and more toward "mere pleasure" rather than strengthening them by making them more useful (23). The purpose of the man of letters is diametrically opposed to the goal of the prince, who, in order to retain his power, wants his subjects to be "blind, ignorant, spiritless, deceived, and oppressed," while the writer hopes that his work brings to the people "light, truth, and pleasure." The actual goal of the man of letters is glory, yet there cannot be real glory without usefulness for the majority of the people.

Alfieri will rate an author as really great only if he has succeeded according to this criterion. How the writer can achieve this utility is, in great measure, determined by his ability to uphold "reason" and "truth." Again and again Alfieri will elaborate on these principles.

The author puts a particular effort into rendering his concepts more concrete. He relies constantly on historical examples, obviously patterning his procedure on the earlier work by Niccolò Machiavelli (1469-1527) Il Principe (The Prince). Conceptually, the essay culminates in the tenth chapter of the third book, which affirms the superiority of the literary word even over law, when the aim is to "confirm healthy public opinion" through reason and truth. It is easier, he says, to instill some truth in "the hearts of a multitude by presenting it as entertainment in a play which everyone understands and enjoys rather than by a public speech" (24). After two short chapters, the book concludes by restating the overall importance of the twin principles of delight and utility, stressing the fact that, since every moral truth is hostile to all illegitimate power, letters can only flourish in a climate of liberty.

True to these principles, Alfieri dedicated his

treatise On Tyranny to liberty. This work is yet
another example of Alfieri's rationalistic poetics.
Again he states that he is attempting to elucidate his
thoughts with precision, simplicity, and clarity. His
wish is to develop only the truths consonant with reason.
The statement and the desire are reminiscent both of the
first chapter of Machiavelli's Prince and of the neoclassical aesthetics of Alfieri's time (25).

As a whole, On Tyranny is not as inspiring a work as
The Prince and Letters. It contains many of the cli-
chés about tyranny common to the eighteenth century. To
the reader of Alfieri's tragedies, it is nonetheless a
useful instrument, for it places in focus the figure of
the tyrant. The third chapter illustrates the fact that
tyranny is based on "fear." Fear is experienced not only
by the oppressed, but by the oppressor. The tyrant's
terror stems from the knowledge he has of the enormous
distance between his "imagined" power and his actual
weakness (26). The portrait of the tyrant we derive from
this presentation is that of a man who trembles in his
palace at the very thought of how deep a hatred his bound-
less power must inspire in everybody's heart. The tyrant
trembles also at the very mention of the word justice.
Everything that appears to be dictated by reason arouses
his suspicions: he fears good citizenship; he can never
feel safe unless the most important matters of business
are conducted by his "trusted" men—that is, by men like
himself—but still more cruel, more unjust, and still
more possessed by fear.

The postulate supporting these principles is that
human nature fears and abhors anything—anybody—that
might mean harm, even though the harm is justly determined. Moreover, any unlimited power, by being a nefarious usurpation of the natural rights of man, instills a
deep terror of his capability to hurt one and all.
Alfieri's tyrant, in his complexity, is a man isolated at
the top of the pyramid of power, a solitary and vulner-
able figure.

Philip subsumes all the essential elements of
Alfieri's poetics, from the division into five acts, the
elimination of confidants, props, and so forth to the
technique of the soliloquy, as well as incorporating his
particular conceptualization of the tyrant. Alfieri
created the character of Philip to give substance to a
figure he abhorred and, at the same time, found fascinating in his innate tragic dimension of solitude. Even

Philip's wife and son are seemingly his enemies. He can
rely only on Gomez, the basest of abject courtiers. The
palace is a nest of intrigue and deceit. Under the pretext of the so-called "reason of state"—the expression
recurs twice in the second scene of the second act—
Philip suspects and condemns his son. Is he "happy"?
His last words confirm and seal his constant state of
uncertainty, suspicion, and fear, but the consciousness
of it appears well before the last words:

> O wretched lot of kings! They cannot utter,
> Tremble to utter, much less dare obey,
> Nature's benign affections. Nay, so far
> From even daring to make mention of them,
> They are compell'd, by interest of state
> To stifle and dissemble utterly
> Natural impulses.
>
> [2.2]

If Alfieri's treatises deal theoretically with the
institution of monarchy, identifying the king as merely
the modern version of the tyrant, the tragedies dramatize
the conflict in individuals. The classical dramatic tradition had clearly established how effective, indeed
tragic, is the intermingling of family affairs with interests of state. The dialectic tension deriving from such
situations is potentially tremendous, and practically all
of Alfieri's works will seek their generating force in
it.

Philip's words to Carlos exemplify his consciousness
of his dual role and its divisive power:

> Approach me, Prince. Now tell me, when dawns
> That day in which, with the fond name of son,
> Thy father may accost thee? Then should'st see,
> (Ah, would'st thou have it so!) combined together
> The name of father and of king; ah, why,
> Since thou lov'st not the one, fear'st not the other?
>
> [2.4]

Although Philip is being (or thinks he is) subtly deceitful, he is a victim of his own prerogative, like all
tyrants, and therefore just as oppressed, in an absolute
sense, as his subjects. The oedipal rivalry between
father and son, which in private citizens would mainly be
concerned with securing the affection (possession) of the

wife-mother, is here complicated by the political struggle, the conquest of power or its retention.

Philip satisfies the requirements of both the "useful" and "pleasurable." A powerful tragedy, well-
written, built on a strong, yet simple structure, it
never slackens in pace, nor deviates from its main line
of action. From the point of view of its message, the
play aspires to teach the love of liberty and of personal
dignity. It aspires to fire a hatred of tyranny, the
inevitable outcome of all power in the mind of the
author. Not too many years later Ugo Foscolo (1787-1828)
would immortalize Alfieri in his poem Dei Sepolcri (On
Sepulchres) for achieving just such goals. We would
like, however, to include Alfieri in the words of praise
that Foscolo dedicated to Machiavelli in the same poem.
According to Foscolo, Machiavelli

> humbling the proud sceptres of earth's kings,
> Stripped thence the illusive wreaths, and showed the
>   nations
> What tears and blood defiled them . . .

In these lines it is suggested that Machiavelli, under
the pretext of giving practical advice to the princes of
his time, was in reality making it known to everybody on
what evil deeds power is founded (27). Foscolo's intuition was not only in joining the great Florentine and the
great Piedmontese in his imaginary line of geniuses, it
was also in calling up the idea of a secret affinity
between the two. In fact, his praise of Machiavelli's
Prince applies to Alfieri's Philip and to his theater
in general.

Chapter Two
The Heroics of Pessimism

Some of the blemishes that Alfieri was prepared to
acknowledge in his Philip were determined, at least
partially, by what he called the "modernity" of the
historical facts on which the play was based (1). He
felt that characters such as Philip and Don Carlos had
not yet been consecrated by tradition and, therefore,
were lacking the dignity and majesty of Oedipus, Orestes,
and similar figures of the Greek theater. He quickly
turned to more classical themes: the tragedies immediately following Philip treat Greco-Roman subject matter.

Polinice (Polynices) was devised in 1775, like
Philip, and published in 1783. Inspired by the reading
of Statius's Thebaid, it centers on the two brothers
Eteocles and Polynices (2). The main themes are their
ambition for absolute power and the curse of mutual insa-
tiable hatred cast on them by the gods as a punishment
for the incest committed by their parents, Oedipus and
his mother Jocasta. Closer to Alfieri's time, the theme
had been treated again by the French classical dramatist
Racine (1639-1699) in his Thébaide ou Les Frères Enne-
mis (The Hostile Brothers) (3). Alfieri had at first
given his play the same title as Racine's. Later he
changed it to Polinice e Eteocle (Polynices and
Eteocles), to Tebaide (Thebaid), and finally to
Polynices (4).

The two brothers had agreed to reign over Thebes alternately for one year each. The drama ensues when Eteocles
breaks the pact and refuses to step down. Polynices,
who, during his brother's year of rule had been outside
the country, has married Argeia, daughter of Adrassus,
King of Argos, and is now coming back at the head of the
Argian army to claim his throne. Jocasta, the mother of
the two antagonists, and Antigone, their sister, also
take part in the action. So does Creon, the uncle, who
is trying to exploit the situation to his own advantage.
The plot moves forward toward the reciprocal slaying of

Eteocles and Polynices through intermittent possibilities
of peace between the two. Jocasta's forebodings of doom
and Creon's scheming make up a dramatic backdrop for the
main characters.

Alfieri's originality consisted, in this case, in
giving Polynices a somewhat nobler character than his
brother's. He made him capable not only of hating, but
of loving as well. Polynices is the one who has succeeded in breaking out of the fatal boundaries of the
accursed city. By going away, he has discovered the love
of a wife and a son. Polynices was also the one ready to
observe the pact, unlike Eteocles.

Eteocles, however, emerges as the most fascinating
character. It is he who displays the strongest emotions
in his relentless quest for power: "My existence and my
throne are one" [1.2]. Polynices, on the other hand,
appears weakened by a sense of piety, this in spite of
the curse that weighs upon him as much as it does upon
his brother. Jocasta is a very dramatic figure as the
mother, who, no matter what, cannot help but love her two
sons equally; her inner conflict has no solution. This
element of feminine despair is complemented and heightened by Antigone, a touching character whose potential
will emerge fully in another tragedy bearing her name.

If the action of Polynices is structured with the
two brothers on one side and the two women on the other,
Creon makes up its connective tissue. A major ingredient
of the action is the force of fate. Predestination (a
major theme in Alfieri's tragedies of Greek inspiration)
is more than just an imposition of the classical subject
matter. Its urge allows Alfieri to avoid, at least
partially in this play, the all-too-obvious intrusions of
Philip's heavy political theorizing. The poet's intimately pessimistic vision of reality is now embodied in a
force stronger than any single individual. The symbol of
everything adverse to man's aspirations in life, fate,
ultimately crushes him—his willful efforts notwithstanding. The author appropriates both the rich classical
heritage and the Romantic sense of impotence precipitated
by the waning of the Enlightenment's optimism (5). The
thirst for power, typical of Alfieri's tyrants, faces a
new adversary, over and above the practical obstacles
raised by political reality. It is the adversary that
everyone carries within himself. Alfieri will make this
fully understood in his best works, Saul and Mirra.

The two plays, Polynices and Antigone, uncover a

pessimistic truth about human destiny, which will later
echo in the poetry of Giacomo Leopardi (1798-1837). The
bitter realization that one is "reprobated long before
one's birth" is uttered by the protagonist of Antigone
at the very beginning of the tragedy. The sense of predestined doom, then, is expressed through a feminine character—just as the most anguishing accents of Polynices
are voiced by Jocasta for having given birth to two such
brothers. Here, while the two men are absorbed in the
retention or acquisition of power, the women are battling
with feelings of guilt and doom. The dramatic culmina-
tion of Polynices, however, belongs unequivocally to
Eteocles. To the very end he is devoured by hate and by
the spirit of revenge. He incarnates the classical sense
of fate Alfieri had made his.

Polynices' noble offer of forgiveness is anachronis-
tically tinged with a Christian sense of piety. Such a
component works counter to the effectiveness of the character. It may perhaps be explained by Alfieri's belief
in the moral dimension of poetry, already inherent incidentally in Aeschylus's ancient tragedy insofar as it
condemns incest.

In the last scene of the most dynamic fifth act
Eteocles dies from a blow delivered (unwillingly) by
Polynices, but, feigning a reconciliation with his
brother, he stabs him with his dagger:

> I yield. Come, then, O brother, to the arms
> Of thy expiring brother, slain by thee . . .
> Come, and receive in this my last embrace . . .
> Brother . . . from me . . . the death thou meritest.
>
> [5.3]

The dark note he strikes in dying, "I am revenged. I
die, and still I hate thee . . . ," is consistent with
what Eteocles had already expressed in the strongest
terms. It is the sense of damnation imposed on them both
by the gods, a sense of guilt he felt in his blood, in
his whole being: "nor though my blood is lost, that my
foul veins / of their inbred and cleaving hate are
cleansed. . . ." Since Alfieri had chosen to eliminate
the chorus from his works, the dramatic finale is com-
mented upon directly by Jocasta. All of the built-up
tension that led to the reciprocal slaying of the two
brothers is now concentrated on the figure of the incestuous mother. Doom and guilt had possessed her throughout

the action: they now explode forcefully. She challenges
the gods, her words ringing with the courage of despera-
tion, with the pride of one who has nothing more to lose:

> Behold the work complete:
> These sons of incest, these unnatural brothers,
> Murder each other: here behold a mother,
> To whom there nothing now remains to lose.
> Ye gods, than us more guilty, from your skies
> Crush me will all your bolts: or ye're no gods.

[5.3]

The gods do not heed her injuction, and after she faints
into Antigone's arms, the action is concluded with the
daughter's cry of "Mother!"

The existential drama of the individual fighting
forces far above any possibility of control is further
intensified with Antigone (6). This play is both a
continuation of the preceding action and a more successful interpretation of a hopeless situation, or predestined catastrophe. The plot centers around Antigone's
determination to give burial to Polynices' remains
against the will of Creon, now king of Thebes. More
poetically suggestive than Polynices, the drama is contained in one main character—a feminine figure of a much
more delicate nature than either Polynices, Eteocles, or
even Jocasta. This is actually a tragedy of women, for
the femininity of Antigone is complemented by that of
Argeia, Polynices' widow. Although Alfieri regarded the
figure of Argeia as practically superfluous, her presence
is in fact very effective in its amplification of
Antigone's feelings (7). Of the four protagonists (the
other two are Creon, in the role of despicable tyrant,
and Haemon, his son, who is in love with Antigone),
Argeia alone will be spared and will go back to her native Argos. Both Antigone and Haemon will perish, crushed
by a fatal destiny, here personified by Creon (8).

Antigone is freed from the cliché of the helpless
victim by her awareness that rather than a mere prisoner
of Creon's tyrannical will, she is the victim of a preor-
dained order of things. At the beginning, when she tells
Argeia about the tragic death of her brothers, the suicide of her mother, and the pitiful condition of Oedipus,
she draws a sharp distinction between herself and her
sister-in-law. Argeia should go on living. She,
Antigone, is possessed by her own will to die:

> Argeia, I will not dispute with thee
> About our love; thy death I will oppose.
> Thou art a widow; what a husband thou
> Hast lost, I know; but thou like me, of incest
> Are not the fruit; thou hast a mother still;
> Like mine, thy father is not blind, or outcast;
> Nor—worse than all these—a guilty father.
>
> [1.3]

In her eyes, Creon appears merely as an instrument of
fate. She seems not fearful, but definitely superior to
him. Her words to Argeia are sculpted in determination:
"Take no offense, if I would die alone / Here I was born,
my life forfeited."

A measure of her strength in facing the adversity of
fate is given by her renouncing marriage to the man she
loves. Creon fears the people's reaction should Antigone
die; he is ready to spare her life, provided she marries
his son, Haemon. This would bind her more directly to
him and would strengthen his reign, but Antigone refuses.
She could not marry the son of the man who has brought
about the destruction of her family, and she is aware of
her destiny of expiation. The full weight of the curse
imposed by the gods on the incestuous family falls on a
lonely feminine character, who offers her own person as
the scapegoat in the ritual of placating their wrath.
What could have become a melodramatic situation, resting
on a feeling of pity for the sacrifice of a helpless victim, is turned into the admirable tragedy of one undaunt-
ed soul, who is ready to renounce everything. She tells
Haemon to beg his father not for her life, but for her
death; the depth of her despair is such that the funereal
request appears as a last pledge of love:

> Haemon obtain my death; 'twill be a pledge,
> The only one I can accept, of love.
>
> [3.2]

Antigone's will is so strong, her determination so
unfaltering, that it dominates the whole action. Even
Haemon is swept along by Antigone's fatal force; from it
he will derive the strength to perform the ultimate act
of self-assertion: that of killing himself.

Again, the challenged authority is not only that of a
tyrant, but that of the father as well. In the exchange
that takes place when Haemon, in order to free his be-

loved Antigone, confronts his father Creon, the word
son changes its intonation frantically from fatherly
tenderness to filial resentment:

> Creon: Son, what is thy intent?
> Haemon: Call me not son!
>   I have no father. Of a tyrant king
>   I come to abrogate the impious law.

[5.6]

Inasmuch as Creon's reaction is reminiscent of similar
confrontations between Philip and Don Carlos ("Against
thy father . . . and against thy king / Thou, thou in
arms?"), it connects with the archetype of Alfieri's
dramatic conception. Haemon is shown the body of
Antigone, slain by the king's soldiers. He is on the
verge of striking his father with his sword, but then he
turns it upon himself. His last words to Creon reiterate
the motif of their tormented relationship:

> I was . . . to thee a son . . . Thou never wert
> Never . . . to me . . . a father . . .

[5.6]

While such dramatic scenes fulfill their theatrical
purpose quite effectively in the theater, on closer analysis Haemon's resentment sounds somewhat forced, as his
last words are dictated by feelings that we were given no
reason to suspect he harbored in his heart. Alfieri
wanted, at all costs, to stress the hatred that the
tyrant generated, even in his own son. Notwithstanding
the specific similarity of the father-son confrontation,
Creon's situation is made diametrically opposite to that
of Philip by his love for Haemon. In the end, immersed
in the blood he has caused to be spilled, the tyrant
remains isolated by his own power. Here, Alfieri's concept of fatality effectively blends with his concept of
tyranny.

In her struggle with fate Antigone is the most successful character in the tragedy, though her human opponent,
Creon, is equally well drawn—an intensely dark figure
who relentlessly follows his goal of power. Argeia simply adds a touch of delicate femininity; Haemon's contribution to the action is more conceptual than political.
By contrast, he serves the purpose of throwing into
relief Antigone's strength of character. In essence,

Alfieri's Antigone rests on a dramatic "dialogue" between two antithetical personages, Antigone and Creon.
As in Alfieri's best achievements, the more touching and
psychologically complex of the two antagonists is the
feminine one.

Agamemnon and *Orestes*

Agamennone (Agamemnon) and Oreste (Orestes)
were conceived by Alfieri on the same day—May 19, 1776.
Because of the proximity of their "birth" and the unity
of their subjects, the author was prompted to refer to
them as the "twin tragedies" (9). As far as the conceptual components (and particularly the theme of revenge) are
concerned, Agamemnon and Orestes pursue the inspira-
tional line of Antigone, while Virginia (which, in
fact, was written between Antigone and the twin tragedies) marks a thematic shifting. In commenting on them
before Virginia, we intend to emphasize a continuity in
Alfieri's concern with the power of fate. The first
title for Agamemnon had been The Death of Agamemnon,
but in his striving for expression, the author settled
for the simpler form, which had already been adopted by
the time of the first versification (1778), and retained
through the second, stylistic elaboration (1781). The
Hellenic plot is inspired by the tragedies of Aeschylus
filtered through the reinterpretation of the Latin poet,
Seneca, noted for his rhetorical insistence on the hor-
rific and gruesome aspects of the story. Although at the
time Alfieri had in fact been studying and translating
Seneca intensely, he felt that his works owed nothing to
him but their initial inspiration (10).

Clytemnestra dominates the action. The tragedy could
very well have been named after her. Once more the dark
forces of fate constitute the dynamics of this drama's
rather simple plot. While Agamemnon is leading the Greek
armies against Troy, his wife Clytemnestra has fallen
prey to a blinding passion for Aegisthus, son of the
incestuous Thyestes and his daughter, Pelopia. Aegisthus
is seeking revenge against Agamemnon, whose father,
Atreus, had murdered Thyestes' children and driven him to
suicide. Haunted by Thyestes' ghost, Aegisthus induces
Clytemnestra to assassinate her husband upon his return,
in spite of Electra's attempts to detach her mother from
such a perfidious lover.

Agamemnon is a rather passive figure, and Electra
functions mainly as her mother's conscience: the true
protagonists are Clytemnestra and Aegisthus.   It is a
peculiar and original feature of this drama that these
two characters are ambiguously on the same side of the
fence.   They have a common goal in crime: for Aegisthus,
it means avenging a wrong done to his family; for
Clytemnestra, it means murdering her husband and king.
The analytical unfolding of Clytemnestra's wavering feelings, down to the moment of her last nefarious deed, constitutes the backbone of the dramatic body of the play.
The forces of fate besieging Clytemnestra are clearly
incarnated by her lover who, in turn, is himself the
instrument and victim of those forces.   An impressive
inner process takes place in the character of Aegisthus
as well.

Paradoxically, the conquest of the throne of Argos
becomes almost incidental.   As thirst for power is not
the motor of this tragedy, what operates dynamically
within Aegisthus is the search for the liberation and
fulfillment he experiences with the death of Atreus's
son:

>   Come forth,
> Thyestes, from profound Avernus; come,
> Now is the time: within this palace now
> Display thy dreadful shade.   A copious banquet
> Of blood is now prepared for thee, enjoy it:
> Already o'er the heart of thy foe's son
> Hangs the suspended sword; now, now he feels it:
> An impious consort grasps it: it was fitting
> That she, not I, did this: so much more sweet
> To thee will be the vengeance, as the crime
> Is more atrocious . . .
>
>   [5.3]

The hammering repetition of the adverb now expresses
the exultance of the accomplished revenge.   The shade of
his father is placated and ceases to oppress and torment
him.   New fears, it is true, will come later from another
and more tangible source: the cluster of themes to be
developed in Orestes.

Even though the author concentrates his attention on
the process of the queen's perdition, the double line of
dénouement we have referred to is the structural axis of
the tragedy.   From the very beginning a strong sense of

fatality is expressed by both Clytemnestra and Aegisthus.
Alfieri, by again employing the procedure of the soliloquy, allows his two main characters to voice their drama.
Thyestes' ghost, thirsty for revenge, dominates Aegisthus's imagination:

> O bloody, angry, discontented shade
> Of unavenged Thyestes, why pursue me?
> Leave me, oh father; . . . go; depart from hence,
> Once more return thou to the Stygian shores.
> All, all thy furies fill my breast; thy blood,
> Too surely runs through all my veins. I know
> That I am the offspring of flagitious incest,
> To guilt predoom'd.
>
> [1.1]

Clytemnestra's fragility, on the other hand, is rendered
not so much by her expressing any precise determination
to accomplish a particular action, but rather by her sub-
mission to the dictates of fate:

> And who am I?
> Am I not Leda's daughter? Helen's sister?
> A blood impure as theirs runs in my veins.
> The will of angry gods, an unknown force,
> Are dragging me along, despite myself.
>
> [1.3]

Her words echo Aegisthus's attributing his predestination
to his tainted and guilty blood, and they seem to form
the cohesive force that binds the two together in a
common destiny.

Once having promised revenge to his father's ghost,
Aegisthus asserts that, since he cannot use force, he
will have recourse to cunning—"I must have recourse to
art before / I use the sword"—or, as Machiavelli would
have put it, he will employ the qualities of the fox, not
those of the lion. Alone and powerless, Aegisthus has at
his disposal, nonetheless, the most effective weapon he
could want, Clytemnestra, and he turns his deceitful art
to work upon her will. The tragedy of a mind overcome by
a fatal passion draws its power from Alfieri's paramount
concept of life, always tinged by the same pessimistic
outlook.

In the following century the great novelist Alessandro
Manzoni (1785-1873), drawing his inspiration from histori-

cal circumstances, created in The Betrothed the character of the "Nun of Monza," who might be termed a "Romantic" sister to Clytemnestra. The nun's will is forced
twice. Conditioned by her father to "spontaneously"
choose the veil, she is then seduced by a man who leads
her to sin and crime. Both women struggle against forces
that inexorably repel and attract them. In both cases an
illegitimate passion for a deceitful man fulfills their
destiny.

Alfieri was not always the best critic of his own
works. In the case of the personage of Clytemnestra,
while he recognized that the character was psychologically sound when seen against the background of Greek emphasis on predestination, he objected that, rationally,
nobody would accept her insane passion for a worthless
individual, nor her rejection of a great king (11). But
what could be more human, and even rational, than a woman
whose husband has been gone for years taking a lover? In
the particular case of Agamemnon's wife, matters had
worsened even before the king's departure, for in order
to assure safe sailing to the Greek fleet, he had sacri-
ficed their daughter, Iphigenia, to the gods.

Cleverly working on Clytemnestra's sympathies,
Aegisthus emphasizes his own downtrodden social status as
compared to the glorious Agamemnon. He describes himself
as "the branch obscure of a detested blood"; a man "deprived of glory, wealth, arms, subjects and friends."
Clytemnestra retorts that he is also free of crime:

> 'Tis true thou graspest not
> The sceptre of Atrides; but the dagger,
> Trickling and reeking with my daughter's blood,
> I see not in thy hands. Ere from my breast
> He dared to wrest my daughter, and to drag her
> A bleeding victim to the impious altar . . .

[1.2]

In the Greek world Clytemnestra was interpreted as
exemplifying the unfaithful wife, while her counterpart,
Penelope, represented the exemplary spouse who remained
true to her husband, Ulysses, during his long years of
absence. The peculiarity of the case resides not so much
in Clytemnestra taking a lover, but rather in her choice.
That was the work of fate: to have fallen in love with
the cursed son of Thyestes.

Aegisthus's art is subtle, but his sly revenge becomes

more horrid by having Agamemnon killed by his own unfaithful wife. The extreme nature of his guilt and
Clytemnestra's own tragic fate are sealed the moment she
unconditionally and blindly agrees to share her lover's
destiny:

> Ere that hour comes,
> I will inseparably join our fates.
> Thy frank and modest language hath inflamed
> My bosom more than ever: more and more
> I see thou 'rt worthy of a better fate.

[1.2]

Her ultimate mistake is in her blindness. Unaware that
no mortal can alter his lot in life, she regards her
lover as worthy of a different destiny from the one the
gods have imposed on him. Nothing succeeds in freeing
her from her passion: not Agamemnon's magnanimity in
sparing Aegisthus, nor Electra's advice. Rather than
lose Aegisthus when he is ordered to leave Argos,
Clytemnestra murders her spouse.

Aegisthus never tells her directly to do so. Rather,
he lets her reach the frightful decision on her own. By
the beginning of the fourth act the process of channeling
her will in the desired direction is completed:

Aegis.   Another plan, perchance, e'en now remains . . .
           But little worthy . . .
Cly.   And it is?
Aegis.   Too cruel.
Cly.   But certain?
Aegis.   Certain, ah, too much so!
Cly.   How
           Canst thou then hide from me?
Aegis.   Of me demand it?
Cly.   What then may it be? . . .

Finally, with an outburst of passion, she recognizes what
had been germinating in her mind all along:

Cly.   Now I understand thee. What a
           flash,
           O what a deadly, instantaneous flash
           Of criminal conviction, rushes through
           My obtuse mind! What throbbing turbulence
           In ev'ry vein I feel! I understand thee:

> The cruel remedy . . . the only . . .
> Is Agamemnon's life-blood.
>
>   [4.1]

Clytemnestra's last doubt is easily, and ironically, dis-
pelled by Aegisthus, who suggests that Agamemnon wants to
make Cassandra—whom he has brought back enslaved from
Troy—his mistress. The human condition, which Alfieri
sees as plagued with impotence whenever confronted by the
blind fury of outside forces, appears at this moment in
all its weakness. Aegisthus deploys the banal weapon of
jealousy on a wife who is unfaithful and who despises her
husband:

> Cly.   What said'st thou? . . .
>   Cassandra chosen as my rival? . . .
> Aegis.   So
>   Atrides wills.
> Cly.   Then let Atrides perish.
> Aegis.   How? By what hand?
> Cly.   By mine, this very night,
>   Within that bed which he expects to share
>   With this abhorred slave.
> Aegis.   O Heav'ns! but think . . .
> Cly.   I am resolved . . .
>
>   [4.1]

Clytemnestra's resolution is carried out, and her tragic
fate is sealed forever.
     Orestes develops the action of Agamemnon after a
ten years' lapse has occurred. Alfieri believed that the
"twin" tragedies, being so closely related to each other,
should be represented on two consecutive nights (12).
The characters are now five; Orestes and his faithful
friend Pylades take the place of Agamemnon; the other
three—Electra, Aegisthus, and Clytemnestra—remain the
same. In practice, however, they are still four, as
Pylades is so closely tied to Orestes as to give the
impression of being merely his alter ego. Pylades' function in the unfolding drama is mainly that of tempering
his companion's impetuosity—while at the same time put-
ting it into sharper relief. The setting is the same,
and, as in the preceding work, the forces of fate pres-
sure the characters toward revenge. Aegisthus now reigns
in Argos, sharing the throne with Clytemnestra, who has
become his wife. The action begins on the anniversary of

Agamemnon's death, at night, when we espy Electra steal-
ing out secretly to honor her father's tomb.

By the second scene of the first act the attention
shifts to Clytemnestra, who is crushed with sorrow and
remorse. Orestes and Pylades arrive furtively in Argos;
they meet Electra, who rejoices when she recognizes her
brother, Orestes, and even more because she sees him as
an instrument of revenge. In order to carry out their
plan, keeping their identity a secret, the pair of
friends claim to be the bearers of the news of Orestes'
accidental death in a chariot race. Clytemnestra believes the story and falls into despair. Aegisthus is
suspicious, especially when confronted with Orestes' boldness and obvious contempt, and has them imprisoned.
Electra fatally reveals their true identity, and
Aegisthus exults. However, before their death sentence
can be carried out, the people of Argos rise in revolt.
Orestes and Pylades are set free and pursue Aegisthus.
In the end, the son of Agamemnon slays him, and in so
doing, blinded not so much by darkness as by fury, he
slays Clytemnestra as well.

Is the figure of Orestes a re-edition of the Alfierian
hero? There is one basic element that differentiates him
from the typical antagonist of a tyrant. Orestes is not
motivated by high, noble, political ideals, and not even
by thirst for power. His motivations are at the same
time extremely personal and determined by fate. The
blood of Agamemnon calls him, as it were, to action. He
has, however, the forte sentire of the Alfierian hero,
the strong feeling and force of character. Alfieri was
well aware of the theatrical potential of such a personality. From the very beginning he depicts Orestes as if he
were possessed by the Furies; as indeed he is in the end,
after his matricide. It was the author's belief that if
the character had been drawn in more subdued tones, it
would have appeared nonverisimilar for him to explode
unexpectedly at the end (13). Essentially, the poetry of
this tragedy is shaped by Alfieri's pessimism concerning
the unequal struggle between the individual and the
obscure forces that assail him from within as well as
from without. Particularly unequal is the struggle of
Clytemnestra's will subjugated to the end by her passion
for Aegisthus, no matter how many conflicting emotions
besiege her heart.

Aegisthus and Electra remain basically the same,
except for the fact that the latter's dramatic potential

is enriched by the spirit of revenge. Nevertheless,
Clytemnestra once more emerges as the most fascinating
figure. Her heart offers fully the measure of the fatal
weakness of human nature, while Orestes may seem more
linear, even though his psychological depth is greater
than appears on the surface. Alfieri was able to enrich
the impact of Clytemnestra's drama and to differentiate
it from the preceding tragedy by emphasizing her double
role as mother of the children of Agamemnon and wife of
their enemy; and also by stressing her torment at not
being able to be either mother or wife. Her situation is
accurately depicted by Electra to Orestes:

> Now wife, now mother; yet ne'er wife or mother:
> Remorseless thoughts, by thousands and by thousands,
> Distract her heart by day; and horrid phantoms
> Scare from her nightly pillow quiet sleep:
> Behold the life she leads.
>
> [2.2]

Such is the lot of Clytemnestra, such the high toll
she has to pay for her crime. The tragedy's dynamic
unity springs from the interplay of dialectically contrasting moods: remorse, pain, sorrow, and a feeling in
Clytemnestra of continual oscillation between love for
Aegisthus and love for her children; a burning determination for revenge in Orestes. Eventually the forces will
collide, and one will destroy the other. Clytemnestra
will find the peace of death, while from that point on
Orestes will be punished for the slaying of his mother by
losing his will to the Furies. Critics have objected
that Orestes appears on the scene with an excessive
charge of passion. We should bear in mind, however, that
the character bears the scars of the traumatic experience
he had undergone ten years earlier. Then, he had witnessed, indirectly, his father's brutal murder at the
hands of his mother—though he had not learned the true
nature of the event till later.

On the night of Orestes' return Alfieri has him relive
the tragic occurrence in a series of powerful flashbacks:

> At last we have arrived.—Here Agamemnon
> Fell massacred; and here Aegisthus reigns?—
> This palace, though I left it but a child,
> I find familiar still. Just Heav'n in time
> Conducts me hither.—Twice five years have pass'd,
> This very night have pass'd, since slain by treason,

My father made these palace walls resound
With mournful cries. O! Well I recall it! . . .

[2.1]

Orestes' ability to recall the minutest details of the
event which took place upon the return of a father he had
never seen before that day and whom he had known only by
fame, demonstrates that the powerful impression was indel-
ible in the character's mind. Exploiting all its theatrical effectiveness and poetical resonance, Alfieri
emphasizes, in the recollection scene, the <u>sound</u>
factor. The most obsessive elements of Orestes' speech
are the cries of the dying Agamemnon, echoed by those of
the child who is being spirited away to safety:

. . . and behind me there <u>resounded</u>
A long <u>confusion</u> of <u>lamenting voices</u>,
Which made me weep, and <u>shriek aloud</u>, and tremble,
I knew not wherefore . . .

[1.1]

The effect of the account is especially impressive
since it is projected against the silence of the night
that envelops Orestes and Pylades. The poignancy of the
situation is enhanced by the fact that the young Orestes
was not yet aware that it was his own father's fate he
was witnessing. The child's crying out takes on the painful aspect of a visceral dialogue between father and son.

Orestes' so fully living again the tragic event provides a motive for the impatience and fury of his yearning for a fateful vengeance. He has traveled back in
time so much as to be immersed again in the same emotions. His feelings are accentuated by the fact that,
after being away for ten years, he returns on the very
anniversary of the fatal event. It is night again, and
all that has filled the intervening years (except for the
hate that has been nurturing) is wiped out of his conscience. He is taken back in space and time; everything
is still the same, but in his hate, he is now a grown
man:

In manhood I return, at length in manhood;
Of hope, of courage, <u>anger</u>, and <u>revenge</u>,
Full I return, whence I departed once,
Weeping, a helpless <u>child</u>.

[2.1]

The superimposition of the desolate child and the angered
adult creates the mesh of psychological dimensions in
which Orestes moves and which determines his behavior
throughout the tragedy.

Some of Clytemnestra's moral ambivalence reverberates
on both Electra and—less—on Orestes.   Her children
would like to love and forgive her, but their filial feeling can hardly blossom while their mother is still
enslaved by her passion for Aegisthus.   In the first
draft of the tragedy Alfieri had accepted Seneca's version of the final scene, and had Clytemnestra slain by
Orestes in the act of trying to shield her lover from her
son's sword (14).   Finally, he altered the Senecan pattern and had her killed, offstage, by an Orestes blinded
by fury and convinced that he is striking out only at
Aegisthus.

The author liked this tragedy, and he was not wrong to
like it.   One particular quality worth underscoring is
the presence of pre-Romantic elements, which are perfect-
ly integrated, and as if redeemed from their usual role
of fashionable background.   The set of imagery induces a
darkly pictorial atmosphere, emerging from the gloom of
the night, the tombs, the blood, the apparition of ghost-
like shades.   Alfieri asserted that he never indulged in
"cheap means," such as these scenario props; nonetheless,
here they are and they create the mood of the drama by being sparingly and adroitly employed.   In this respect,
the first act is where the author sets up the emotional
environment suitable for his tragedy.   The examples are
numerous, and it will suffice to single out a few of them.

By eliminating the chorus, Alfieri redistributed its
function among the characters in the guise of soliloquy.
Electra, in the opening scene, establishes the sinister
tone leading to the unfolding of the action:

> O fatal, horrible, atrocious night,
> O night, forever present to my thoughts!
> Now for two lustres, ev'ry year I've witness'd,
> Pall'd in ensanguined darkness, thy return;
> Yet, 'tis not shed, the blood of expiation,
> The blood that thou requirest.   O remembrance!
> O Agamemnon, my unhappy father!
> Within these thresholds I beheld thee slain;
> And by what hands!   To his most sacred tomb,
> O night, thou guidest me, by all unseen.

[1.1]

When Clytemnestra joins her, Electra intensifies the gloom of the scene by introducing a chromatic note of intense force. She reproaches her mother harshly by throwing images of horror at her:

> Dost thou not see it? On these horrid walls
> Still the coagulated blood-drops stand
> Which thou hast shed: Oh! fly: at sight of thee,
> Behold, it liquifies, and reddens.
>
> [1.2]

—which is reminiscent of Shakespeare's Macbeth, and equally impressive. The horror of the setting is then amplified by Clytemnestra herself. She pours on her daughter all her remorse and sorrow for her crime, almost pushing back to her the same cruel scenes that for her take the shape of obsessive ghosts:

> . . . the ensanguined spectre
> Both day and night before my blasted eyes
> Horribly rises. Wheresoe'er I move,
> Preceding me, the phantom I behold
> Trailing along my desolated path
> A track of sable blood: 'tis on my bed;
> 'Tis on my throne; and worse, 'tis in my heart: . . .
>
> [1.2]

In Agamemnon, Aegisthus's torment is ignited by his father's ghost, finding a liberating appeasement through the murder of the king. For Clytemnestra, liberation can only come with her own demise, and by decree of superior forces. Her inheritance of sorrow is passed on to Orestes.

Chapter Three
The Crisis of Maturity

Virginia and the Other Tragedies of Liberty

Conceived in May, 1777, Virginia was versified between
November of the same year and the month of January, 1778,
but it was given its final form only four years later
(1). These years were crucial for Alfieri's growth as an
author of tragedies. While striving to refine his artistic skill, he struggled to define more clearly the intri-
cate relationship linking his moral, political, and
aesthetical interpretations of reality. The year 1777
marked an intensive study of Machiavelli and Plutarch,
and among the works inspired by these classics Alfieri
singled out three which he liked to refer to as the
"tragedies of liberty": Virginia, Timoleone (Timoleon), and La congiura dei Pazzi (The Conspiracy of
the Pazzi) (2). In these works he tones down the emphasis on fatality, intensifies the moral tone, and creates
a Plutarchian hero who dominates the scene. The hero's
impulses to action are identified in his noble, ideal—
and idealized—nature. His struggles against tyranny may
have different, though invariably tragic, results, but
they are rooted mainly in political opposition, not in
personal rivalries.

Alfieri's compositions tend to overlap in time. As he
was completing a tragedy attuned to a fatalistic and
pessimistic vision of the world, he was able at the same
time to produce works whose dominant mood was vastly
different. In the works written between 1777 and 1781
the subjects alternate between ancient myth and Roman and
Renaissance history. The complexity of the author's
personality and the traits of his ideology are projected
on diverse "realities." His speculative and abstract
concerns are given shape in the various characters and
situations. But the characters are not merely personifi-
cations of ideas. The poet's ambition is, in fact, to
give aesthetic expression to his feelings, moral principles, and political theories, by objectifying them in the
impersonal dimension of history and myth. The varied

production of this period includes also Maria Stuarda (Mary Stuart), Don Garzia, Rosmunda, and Ottavia (Octavia).

Virginia was written right after the treatise On Tyranny. It opens as a world completely different from that of the fatal pessimism we encountered in Agamemnon and Orestes. A new light illuminates the theme, the well-known story is permeated by the aspiration to the highest form of moral and civic virtue. The atmosphere of gloom, the sense of impotence, the graveyard imagery, with all its bloody, ghostly figures, are replaced by a neoclassical splendor. It is almost as if we were look- ing at a newly unearthed Roman frieze, or a statuary group of classically posed figures. The characters of Virginia appear well rounded; they gleam with all the nobility of the type of virtue for which Alfieri was so nostalgic. Unfortunately, their very classical beauty tends to make them appear artificial; they lack the poeti- cal afflatus that could—should—give them life, or at least make them more believable. How much more humanly complex a figure is Clytemnestra than Virginia! Of course, Alfieri felt that his characters had the guaran- tee of historical reality, the credibility of events "as they really happened." Yet, however moved he was by the true source of history, his inspiration was his dwelling on dreams of virtue and spiritual nobility. This charac- teristic, which Virginia has in common with several other plays of the same period, provides insights for the understanding of the author.

The simple plot of Virginia is appropriately concen- trated on the moment of crisis. Although the characters are still few, Alfieri has extended the cast. The six main actors include Virginia; her parents, Numitoria and Virginius; Icilius, the husband-to-be; Appius, who, as chief of the Decemvirs then governing Rome, stands for the figure of the tyrant; and his henchman, Marcus. A chorus of Roman people and soldiers complete the cast.

Appius has been trying unsuccessfully to seduce Virginia and orders Marcus to abduct her. Claiming that Virginia is actually one of his slaves, whom Numitoria had somehow obtained when she was an infant and passed off as her daughter, the crafty Marcus claims her. Rebuked, he hypocritically appeals to Roman law—accord- ing to which Appius must be the arbiter of the case. Icilius, a former tribune, and Virginius, a valiant and respected soldier, are both strong, fearless plebeians;

they both love Virginia and Rome. In their fearless
fight and denunciation of tyranny, they are the true
heroes of the drama, the embodiment of the undying Roman
<u>virtus</u>. Betrayed at last, Icilius fights gallantly,
single-handedly against many, till finally he turns his
sword against himself. When Virginius sees that all is
lost, he slays his daughter in front of the Roman people,
who then storm Appius and his men.

The author felt that a more noble, grandiose, terrify-
ing, and pitiful case than this could not be found. He
felt that all the passions determining such an event were
real, natural, and terrible. Nothing was borrowed from
religion, government, imagination, nor from destiny. He
also saw the event made even greater because it took
place among the Romans, "the most sublime people that
ever existed" (3). The deeds that appealed to his nature
and fascinated him by their greatness, he could no longer
see performed in the contemporary world, populated by
what he regarded as a morally bankrupt humanity; hence,
the escape into a highly idealized world. The moral tone
of the tragedy is established from the very beginning by
both the setting and characters. The setting is the
Roman Forum, the voice is Virginia's:

> O Mother, when I pass
> This Forum, recollection deep and lofty
> Delays my progress. It was in this place
> That herewhile thunder'd from Icilius' lips
> The sentiment of liberty; but now
> Absolute pow'r long since has made him mute.
> How just are both his anger and his grief.
>
> [1.1]

The mere act of passing through the Forum induces
lofty thoughts in Virginia's mind—that is, in Alfieri's.
He is the one who is visited by the spirit of the place,
the one who is inflamed to eloquence by it, and who displays an admirable power of synthesis. In a few verses
he is capable of conveying the essence of the drama:
endangered liberty. It is a futile effort to try to dis-
tinguish between private and public "liberty": the one
entails the other—and vice versa.

Quite effective, theatrically, is the device of starting the action in a moment of joy for Virginia—and for
those who are close to her. She is looking forward to
marrying Icilius, although her joy is soon to be brutally

crushed by Appius's scheming. From then on, the struggle
will be between Icilius—supported by Virginius—and
Appius, the oppressor. The other figures, such as
Virginia and Numitoria, serve mainly as a means to expand
the register of poetical sensibility. Naturally,
Virginia, as the worthy daughter of one of the noble
heroes of the tragedy, and the bride-to-be of another, is
herself imbued with all the required virtues—and acts
accordingly. But she never possesses the will and determination of some other Alfierian heroines.

What is new in this tragedy are Alfieri's insistent,
open attacks on exaltedness and nobility of rank, here
placed in sharp contrast with that of character. Pro-
nouncements to that effect are repeatedly expressed by
those personages who stand for the great collective soul
of the idealized Roman people. When Numitoria confronts
Marcus—her personal antagonist within the infrastructure
of the drama—she stresses proudly her humble origins:

> Learn that we are plebeians, of a race
> Unsullied; that all violence and fraud,
> From infamous patricians, and their clients,
> May be expected here; . . .

[1.2]

Himself a patrician by birth, Alfieri was fortunate
enough, in fact, to be able to chastise the aristocracy
as a peer, and to criticize the mores of the nobility of
the time with no risk of appearing merely envious. Even
in a tragedy like Virginia, where personal convictions
are projected against a framework of historical references, it is just as true a fact as in a theoretical work
such as On Tyranny.

The author's political ideas surface in Virginia any
time the libertarian characters allude to absolute power
and to the corruptions of the people who accept it.
While Icilius's denunciations are of the same tenor as
Alfieri's speculations, Icilius also shares his disillusionment with the political scene of his time. There is
one basic divergence, however. On the stage, the common
people, touched by the courage displayed by Icilius,
Virginius, and Virginia, are depicted as triggered into
action in the end. This was something Alfieri could only
hope would happen to the Italian people—as indeed it did
—in the future.

Icilius's suicide, furthermore, must be seen as strong-

ly exemplifying the Catonian connotations that the physical sacrifice of self acquires with Alfieri and, later,
with Foscolo. Icilius's act is indeed heroic as a pure
affirmation of personal dignity. It is committed after
he has valiantly fought and slain several opponents; it
is an ultimate show. of defiant superiority. The death of
Virginia at the hands of her father is also the equivalent of a suicide. It conveys here a ritualistic meaning. Her father had once given her life, and now, in a
way, he does so again, for only in death can she become
truly free and acquire the immortality of fame of a civic
heroine. Such a situation is diametrically opposed to
Agamemnon's sacrifice of his daughter Iphigenia.

Alfieri felt that Appius, being a Roman Decemvir,
could not appear as really vile and base. Unfortunately,
he does not appear as a real tragic character, nor as possessed by a strong passion. His fleeting desire becomes,
in the end, more like a case of pique; he seems to act
mainly out of injured pride. Vaguely anticipating
Manzoni's Don Rodrigo, he falls short of any tragic fas-
cination he might have had and remains chiefly an
abstract personification of tyranny. Nevertheless, Virginia was hailed at the time, and later on, as one of
Alfieri's best works, precisely for the same reasons that
had inspired him to write it (4).

Timoleon

The idealization of the hero of liberty is even more
pronounced in Timoleone (Timoleon). Alfieri takes
the story from Plutarch, thereby conferring again the
guarantee of history upon his poetical creation. The
scene is the city of Corinth in the fourth century B.C.
Timophanes, the leader of the army in wartime, and the
chief of four hundred guards in peacetime, aspires to
seize absolute power over the town. His brother,
Timoleon, who had once saved his life in battle, becomes
his main antagonist. Demariste, their mother, and
Aeschylus—Timophanes' brother-in-law and friend to both
—are the other characters of the drama. The action is
concentrated within the walls of the two brothers' house
and, with the exception of the final slaying of
Timophanes at the hand of Aeschylus, rests entirely on
dramatic dialogues, expressing opposing points of view.

Alfieri was proud of this tragedy's simplicity of

action, and of its being based entirely on the "purity of
this noble passion for liberty" (5). When an influential
critic of his time, Melchiorre Cesarotti, expressed some
reservations as to the paucity of action, and pointed out
the family-quarrel-like structure of the plot, Alfieri
answered that these defects were entirely the fault of
the subject matter, which did not allow him another
choice. Furthermore, he expressed his aversion to introducing unnecessary events into a story that did not con-
tain any—a technique he regarded as boring because it
seemed to him so easy to implement. Such a device, he
said, is pompously defined as "fantasy" by those who do
not know the proper value of words (6).

Alfieri's rebuttal of Cesarotti's criticism provides
another example of the author's predilection for the
poetics of the verisimilar—rationalistic and anti-
baroque in its origins. By this time, he had mastered so
thoroughly his purely theatrical techniques, that he
could keep the action moving even where, paradoxically,
there was hardly any. In Timoleon everything is again
concentrated on the interrelation of feelings. What
transports this work so much onto the plane of the ideal
is the fact that even the tyrant appears endowed with a
sense of greatness.

Somewhat reminiscent of Polynices is the anguish of
the mother, Demariste, as is the thirst for power—and
the willingness to die for it—that we find in Timophanes. The difference, however, is that Timophanes
really loves his brother, Timoleon; not having understood
the absolute passion for liberty the other has, he is
ready to share the seat of power with him. The figure of
Timophanes both humanizes the tyrant and, paradoxically,
makes him more abstract. In his role as "brother" Timophanes is less remote from reality; on the political
level, however, he comes across as a conceptualized
personification of tyranny. The attraction of ambivalence, which Alfieri felt deeply in the person of the
tyrant, is very apparent in Timoleon, almost as if the
author were trying to verify some of Machiavelli's principles by overlaying their pessimistic historical realism
on Plutarch's story. The very first words of the tragedy:

> No, Aeschylus; if at my side the sword
> All stain'd with blood thou seest, to use force
> I am not led by haughtiness of the heart:

The good of all impels me thus to act;
The fame of Corinth which in me has placed
Its delegated pow'r.

[1.1]

are dictated not merely by Timophanes' will to dissimu-
late: they express a sincere effort to justify his conduct, and a yearning to understand the elusive laws of
political reality. The connotations are further reinforced as Timophanes cites the example of Lycurgus of
Sparta:

Was not e'en he constrained to make himself
A tyrant, to demolish tyranny?
Alas, 'tis force alone that can compel
To virtuous actions a degen'rated people.

Aeschylus, however, retorts:

Thou hast that force. May Heav'n direct thee now
To turn it worthily to worthy ends!

It is, in fact, Aeschylus who expresses Alfieri's tragic
perplexity:

Whichever of you two
I hear the last, methinks the truth resides
With him: and yet the truth is one alone.

[2.4]

Timophanes himself voices the author's doubts when a note
of bitterness invades his speech:

What force, then, is it of an adverse fate
Which always causes, if one man shed blood,
The action to be deem'd tyrannical;
While if a number share in shedding it,
'Tis called a deed of justice?

Once again, to his brother's reproaches, Timophanes will
answer:

To thee the government of one seems guilty;
But, if exemplary just, that one
By practice might refute thy theories.

[3.4]

He sounds even more Machiavellian when he adds that everyone will see

> That a prince raised by blood to the throne,
> Can make his people happy with his laws;
> Each man secure; internal peace enjoy'd;
> His subjects' fear enhancing their obedience;
> Strong in himself, the envy of his neighbors.

[3.4]

Timoleon discards these happy images as signs of hypocri-
sy. He then paints for his brother a detailed picture of
the tyrant's sad lot in verses that seem to condense the
prose of the treatise On Tyranny:

> Fears in thy heart, and terror in thine eye;
> Of apprehension, and suspicious thoughts
> Eternal prey; an everlasting thirst
> For blood and gold, and never satisfied;
> Deprived thyself of what thou tak'st from others,
> Sweet peace of mind; to no one in the world
> By blood or friendship join'd; of fetter'd slaves
> The still more fetter'd lord; the first in rank
> The last in heart of all . . . Ah! tremble; tremble:
> Such wilt thou be; if such thou'rt not already.

[3.4]

Ultimately, though, Timophanes reasserts his thirst for
power. The only way to correct him is by the sword.
Liberty must triumph, and sword it will be. Aeschylus
repudiates his friendship and blood ties to Timophanes,
and it is he, who, as a free citizen, slays the tyrant.

According to some other accounts, such as that of the
historian Diodorus, Timoleon himself slew his brother in
the Roman Forum. For Cornelius Nepos, Timophanes was
slain by someone else on Timoleon's orders (7). It would
seem that if Alfieri had followed Diodorus's account, the
action would have gained in tragic power, but he chose
otherwise. Years later, in Paris in 1788, well before
his shock at the sight of the violence of the French Revolution, when he issued a new edition of his works,
Alfieri dedicated Timoleon to Pasquale De Paoli, a Cor-
sican patriot who had attempted to give independence to
his country. The dedication reflects both the author's
heroic vision of the past and his disillusionment with
the present. Paoli appears to Alfieri as one "of those

very few, who having a very correct idea of other times,
of other people, and of other modes of thought, would
have been hence worthy to have been born, and to have
acted, in an age somewhat less effeminate than our own"
(8).

Since it is obvious that those "very few" men included
the author, who prided himself on his correct idea of
other times, of other people, etc., and who often lament-
ed the fact of not having been born in a more "heroic"
age, the self-revealing statement shows the degree of
Alfieri's identification with those figures he regarded
as exemplary. The few lines declare that what really
counts is the deed itself, not the results, and attest to
an interesting evolution of his ideas with respect to the
Machiavellian he was ten years earlier.

The unfortunate outcome of Timoleon's stand links him
to Paoli: "But as certainly it has not rested with you,
that your country was not restored to liberty, not judging myself (as the multitude is accustomed to do) men
from their fortune, but exclusively from their actions, I
deem you fully worthy to hear the sentiments of Timoleon,
as one that can fully feel and understand them" (9). It
is, however, with La congiura dei Pazzi (The Conspiracy of the Pazzi, 1777) that all of Alfieri's themes are
brought together to produce a denser and more persuasive
tragic climate. The political superstructure, the Plutarchian sense of virtus and noble action, the weight
of fate—in the guise of Machiavellian historical
realism—all become one and give life to the character of
Raimondo (Raymond).

The Conspiracy of the Pazzi

With this tragedy Alfieri returns from myth and
ancient history to what he considered "very modern"
times. Although he believed that a subject derived from
recent history tended to detract from a tragedy's effectiveness, the (relative) historical proximity, as well as
the notoriety of the characters involved, actually
increase the dramatic tension of this play. The time of
the action is 1478, and the place is the Medici palace in
Florence. Lorenzo and his brother Giuliano (Julian in
Lloyd's translation) rule the Florentine Republic, and
have acquired—in the eyes of some—what amounts to tyrannical power. The champion of liberty, and their main

antagonist, is Raimondo (Raymond) of the distinguished
Pazzi family. To complicate matters, Raymond is married
to Lorenzo and Julian's sister, Bianca. Guglielmo,
Raymond's father, and Salviati, the Archbishop of Pisa,
are the other characters involved.

Raymond is impetuously plotting to free the republic
from the two tyrants. He has first to convince his
cautious father to take part in the dangerous scheme,
while keeping Bianca ignorant of the situation. Lorenzo
and Julian are mutually complementary characters—one
bold, the other prudent, in accordance with the famous
Machiavellian distinction of the fox and the lion—and
likewise, Raymond and his father complement each other.
Thus, even though the number of the dramatis personae
nominally includes six characters, essentially, the antithetical protagonists are again just two, and the setting
of the drama is typically simple.

Salviati has a limited functional role that is hardly
realized at all. Alfieri must have regarded Lorenzo, the
tyrant, as the main protagonist: according to his usual
compositional pattern, he does not have him appear until
the second act. But Raymond is the essentially tragic
figure of the play, and a worthy companion to Raymond is,
in this respect, Bianca. She heightens the dramatic
intensity of the Conspiracy by highlighting the intimate ties that bind one faction to the other, and at the
same time she tempers the ferocity of the action with her
exquisitely feminine presence. Woven into the larger
canvas, the thread of her personal drama traces her multiple role as wife, mother, and sister.

In the present play the much-favored technique of
the soliloquy is almost nonexistent. Furthermore, since
Alfieri did not deem it verisimilar that great historical figures of the Italian Renaissance would confide
their innermost feelings to their social inferiors,
all the characters are on the same social level, and
another device—that of the confidant—is eliminated.
The author was convinced that only the third and fifth
acts really counted, the others being mostly "chatter";
in fact, only the last act is very impressive (9). It
reaches such a well-orchestrated complexity of action
and feelings—from the historical particular to the
emotional universal—that it leaves the audience
completely satisfied. Moreover, in contrast to other
works, it is not only the last few scenes of the fifth
act that reach this high level of dramatic tension,

rather the whole act is equally impressive.

The heroic tone is established earlier through the set
speeches against tyranny, and the plot has been brought
to the point in which everything is ready for the slaying
of Lorenzo and Julian. As the fifth act opens, it has
become clear that Raymond is the heart of the action, and
Bianca its soul. It is mainly through her eyes that we
perceive all the depth of human emotion analyzed by
Alfieri. Bianca has chosen Raymond's side: "I do not
hate my brothers, no; but I love Raymond only." And she
remains motivated purely by love. Hers is not a blind
passion, a curse of the gods; it is an emotional choice.
It becomes painful only because of the reality of politics. Although Raymond has not revealed the assassina-
tion plot to her, and she is unaware that the designated
day has come, she can nonetheless feel that some ominous
event is about to take place. She has seen it written on
her husband's face during a tormented, sleepless night:

> But yet this long uninterrupted night,
> Which scarcely yet the rising dawn disperses,
> How different, how very different,
> Was it to thee from all preceding nights!
> Not one brief moment did calm sleep descend
> Upon thy weary eyes. Thou closedst them,
> The better to deceive me, but the thick,
> And frequent pantings of thy breast, thy sighs
> Suppress'd by force alternately
> Inflamed with fire, or bathed in hues of death . . .
>
> [5.1]

The description is effective on more than one level.
Through the motifs of Bianca's love for her husband and
the harmony of her soul with his, it reveals Raymond's
inner torment. Hate is not the only force that animates
him, neither is love for liberty. He is tormented by the
fear of what might happen to his beloved Bianca and their
children as a consequence of his action. Bianca's words
evoke the very early dawn and describe in flashes how
Raymond was preparing to face his tragic destiny:

> The shades of night
> Were undiminish'd yet, when thou already
> Hadst leap'd abruptly from thy bed, like one
> Whom unaccustom'd care consumes. Towards me
> Did not I see thee afterwards direct,

> Sighing, thy pitying eyes?   And scarcely risen
> Thy children one by one embrace?—What say I?
> Nay, rather to thy breast a thousand times
> Glue them, devouring them with eager kisses; . . .
>
> [5.1]

The allusion to the children and to the tears that
Raymond sheds—"a man whose eyes are never visited by
tears"—adds a tremendous pathos to the human element of
this tragedy. After his effort to humanize even the
figure of the tyrant, Alfieri now not only tries but succeeds in making less abstract and less rigid his repub-
lican rebels. The invisible presence of the children is
a major component in this episode, the kind of episode
that made the pathos of Dante's Divine Comedy so well
attuned to the taste of Romanticism. In the scene of the
death by starvation of Count Ugolino, in Canto 33 of the
Inferno, for instance, the children's presence turns a
most ferocious representaion into a moving one, all the
while showing how often innocents pay for the sins of
others. When the "others" are their own parents, the
sense of predestined fate is especially strong. In
Dante's work it was implicitly expressed, in Alfieri's it
is clearly spelled out:

> And, if erewhile I wept . . . I wept the fate
> Of the poor children of an outraged father.
> Must I incessantly not weep their birth,
> And their existence?   Hapless little ones!
> What fate in this long death, which we call life,
> Awaits you! . . .
>
> [5.1]

In the economy of the drama Raymond's pessimistic
vision of life is determined by politics. A citizen who
cannot accept tyranny, he expresses sentiments and convictions that are also premonitory of the universal conclu-
sions concerning the problematics of existence that will
later be voiced by the poets Ugo Foscolo (1778-1827) and
Giacomo Leopardi (1798-1837).
   Bianca's precise portrait of her husband becomes more
and more revealing. Nothing escapes her vigilant, loving
eyes. She understands that a fatal day has dawned by
reading in his face

. . . those manifold

> Tremendous workings of thy countenance,
> That in a crowd in quick succession throng,
> Despairing agony, compassion, rage,
> Hatred, revenge, and love.
>
>   [5.1]

Only after Raymond has left, through further allusions
made by his father Guglielmo, does she grasp the full
meaning of her husband's torment. Her reaction, now also
that of the sister of Raymond's intended victims, is
forcefully natural:

> Ferocious souls!
> Dissembling hearts! I could not have believed.

And she will react even more emotionally when Raymond,
returned from his mission, gives her an account of
Julian's death at his own hands:

> O fatal cruelty! . . . O mortal blow! . . .
> How many of us hast thou slain at once!

Here Alfieri's pessimistic view of humanity, both in
its most obscure, innate, fatalistic form, and in its
political projection, come together. When Bianca hears
the cries of "Slay the traitor," and she asks in bewilder-
ment, "The traitor, who?," Raymond simply answers: "The
traitor . . . is . . . the vanquished!" Alfieri never
compressed his complex ideology into a more laconic and
telling formula. The sentence is exemplary of the parsi-
monious dosage of words the author constantly strived to
attain. A stylistic maturity made of a perfect balance
between meaning and expression has been reached; the
dialectical tension always existing between content and
form has been effectively dissolved.
Raymond's suicide is an act of liberation, and also a
manifestation of sheer physical strength. It is intended
to show Lorenzo that if he, Raymond, had attacked him,
the tyrant would now be dead. He strikes himself violent-
ly, as if symbolically slaying Lorenzo. Meanwhile,
Lorenzo maintains that poetical ambiguity with which
Alfieri has been capable all along of investing this dig-
nified historical personage. Thus, the last voice to be
heard in the scene is Lorenzo ordering Guglielmo to be
taken to his punishment, and Bianca to be removed from
the side of her dying husband. Then he adds:

Time alone
Can soothe her grief.—And time alone can prove
That I am not a tyrant, and that these are traitors.

[5.6]

A certain amount of brotherly concern for Bianca blends
with the solemnity of one who knows that his record will
withstand the test of time and history. Alfieri was
aware that few historians, if any, have branded Lorenzo
as a tyrant. He also knew that his would-be assassin,
Raymond, could be redeemed on the stage, and he invested
him with the heroic aura of fierce love for independence
that he himself cherished above all else.

Of the tragedies of "liberty" The Conspiracy of the
Pazzi is the most successful for psychological accuracy,
emotional intensity, and stylistic effectiveness. Just
as Bianca is more real than many of Alfieri's heroines,
so Raymond ranks first, both as a real hero of liberty,
and as a man. He is endowed with the same love for freedom as Icilius and Timoleon, but how much richer his
personality is; how much more complex his soul.

It is easy to say that Alfieri projected his love for
freedom—both personal and political—upon a character
like Raymond. It is a bit more difficult perhaps, but
equally true, to affirm that the poet was also very close
to Lorenzo. This tyrant figure was what Alfieri needed
to express some of his own emotional contradictions. He
is, after all, the ideal type envisioned by Alfieri:
noble, strong, far superior to his fellows, always ready
to assert himself as an individual—at any cost. Lorenzo
thus fills the role of the tyrant without really being
one—at least not a hateful one.

A Tortuous Path

Don Garzia (Don Garcia) also deals with the Medici
family, though with a branch of the family collateral to
that of Lorenzo. Moreover, since the tragedy has some
affinity with the preceding one, we have decided to
insert it in our discussion at this point. It is not a
"tragedy of liberty," but rather a drama of dark intrigue
and murder. The first idea of Don Garcia had been
sketched before the Conspiracy, in 1776, but it was
completed afterwards, in January, 1782 (11). In the
first half of that year so important for the history of

his theater Alfieri, who was living in Rome, rewrote
several of his tragedies. This was also the year in
which he produced his acknowledged masterpiece, Saul.
He was coming to the end of a tortuous creative path that
ran through 1770-1782, and attaining the ripening point
of the second great moment of his poetical activity. In
this crucial period of intense working and reworking
Alfieri also wrote Rosmunda and Octavia, as well as a
completely new version of Merope (the drama that immediately preceded Saul). Between 1781 and 1783 Alfieri
composed five odes, among which was the ode America
libera (Free America), dedicated to George Washington,
and the Etruria vendicata (Etruria revenged), where the
villains are again the Medici. This period of residence
in Rome was a particularly happy moment in his life. He
had rejoined his beloved Countess of Albany, he was satisfied with his work in general, and relatively at peace
with himself (12).

Alfieri had been intrigued by an account he had read,
while in Florence, of the mysterious deaths of Cosimo
de' Medici's sons, Garcia and Giovanni, and that of his
wife, Eleonora. According to the document, Garcia and
Giovanni had had a violent altercation over which one of
the two was entitled to claim a deer during a hunt.
Garcia had stabbed his brother in the thigh, and Giovanni
died a few days later. When Garcia subsequently appeared
before his father to beg humbly for forgiveness, Cosimo,
still angered by the incident, killed him. Eleonora,
heartbroken, died a few hours later. There were other
versions of the story, but, whatever actually happened,
Alfieri was struck by the act of a father killing a son
to avenge the death of another son (13). There can be no
doubt that Alfieri saw in the account another historical
event well suited to exemplify the principles of Aristotle's poetics—specifically, the arousal of pity, which
Alfieri saw as one of the most effective means to make a
tragedy appealing. This always results from the depiction of a struggle, not between persons indifferent to
one another, but between menbers of the same family (14).
Alfieri's critical comment on Don Garcia expresses the
same notion in almost identical terms.

Alfieri sets his fantasy to work on the original story
with mixed results. The introduction of a third brother,
Piero, greatly influences and determines the action of
the play. While Garcia and Giovanni—the latter's name
being changed to Diego—both appear as noble characters,
Piero is the personification of cunning and deceit.

Cosimo (the first grand duke of Tuscany) is the expression of absolute tyranny. He controls not only the state, but his family. His gloomy patriarchal authority, while anticipating Saul's, reminds us also of Philip in Alfieri's first play. Completely dominated by her husband, Eleonora is portrayed as the victim, her motherly predilection for Garcia being the only spark in an otherwise pale character.

At the center of the plot are two "invisible" personae, Salviati and his daughter Giulia, who, however, never appear on stage. The events take place in Pisa. The baroque novel-like tone of intrigue and subterfuge is heightened by the scheming of Piero, who exploits his father's aversion to Salviati. By a trick, Piero has Garcia unwittingly kill his brother Diego, thus opening up for himself (once Garcia too is slain) the path to the seat of power. It is Piero, in short, who plays the role of the fox to Cosimo's lion—and wins.

Garcia is the hero of the drama. His inner torment is precipitated not so much by his programmatic love for liberty, as by his love for Giulia. Giulia (the daughter of Salviati, Cosimo's antagonist) has been imprisoned by Cosimo. Unless Garcia kills her father, she will be slain by Cosimo. The dilemma calls to mind the dramatic situation in some of the "melodramas" of Pietro Metastasio (1678-1782), but Garcia achieves a few moments of truly tragic greatness. One way out would be for the young hero to have recourse to a noble act of self-sacrifice:

> Rather than see that much-loved maiden dragg'd
> To ignominious death; rather than be
> Polluted with her father's blood, I here
> Will kill myself . . .

[3.5]

However, Piero skillfully convinces him that such an act would solve nothing, for then Cosimo would have both Salviati and his daughter tortured and killed. Piero then claims to have arranged for Garcia to surprise Salviati in a dark cave, but instead he plans to send Diego there in Salviati's place. Alone awaiting the fatal hour, in what he calls the "cave of death," Garcia meditates on the cruelty of his destiny:

> . . . Innocence,
> Thou which wert heretofore my only boast,
> Thou art no linger mine: the impious blow

> I have pledged myself to strike . . . And shall
>   I strike it? . . .
> In ev'ry corner of this gloomy cave
> I hear the sound of death; and on myself
> Alone I cannot now that death inflict?
> O cruel destiny! . . . Night's thickest shades
> Already cover all things . . .
>
> [4.4]

The interplay between the classical motif of a destiny incumbent upon mankind, and the intense Romantic atmosphere of the darkened cave, attains a tragic dimension similar to that of Alfieri's best works (Antigone, in particular, and Orestes). This time the situation is not taken over from tradition but has been entirely constructed by Alfieri's imagination, and the enterprise would have achieved greater dramatic effectiveness were it not for the cumbersome apparatus of Piero's machinations. Unfortunately, they are there, and they constitute the weakness of the tragedy as a whole. However, the figure of Cosimo deserves closer scrutiny.

This character was intended to represent the ultimate despot. His tyrannical will is so exacerbated that it aims at the maximum control it can exert. It finds its paroxysmal expression in his speech to Eleonora, who is desperately trying to understand Cosimo's hatred for Garcia. The father invokes treason; as in Philip, his hatred is supplied with a political motivation. In Garcia's case, his noble liberalism brands him as a renegade:

>   . . . He ought
> To speak not only as I speak; but ought
> To think e'en as I think: he who has not
> A nature like to mine, should change it; yes:
> Not simulate, but change it. Of my race,
> And of my realm, I am the head; the soul
> Am I, with which each living creature here
> Is animated.
>
> [2.1]

While they reflect conceptually certain pages of On Tyranny, these words are a particularly visceral expression of the then widely accepted creed that the monarch is the State.

The relationship between Cosimo and Garcia revolves

around an oedipal jealousy of the father toward the son.
It is Eleonora's predilection for Garcia that triggers
Cosimo's resentment. Even though there is no explicit
allusion to incestuous love, subconsciously Cosimo feels
that such a possibility exists, and he openly reproaches
his wife:

> This overweening, ill-placed love,
> More than it ought to do, thy judgment blinds.
> Thou mak'st an idol to thyself of Garcia;
> Save him thou lovest, and thou seest nothing.
> What I call <u>crime</u>, thou dar'st in him call
>   <u>virtue</u>?
> This altercation is not new between us;
> But ev'ry day it more displeases me.
>   [2.1]

Cosimo's figure thus compounds thirst for power, des-
potic will, and a seething sense of rivalry toward his
wife's favorite son. But even though the villain seems a
more intriguing character than the hero, his lack of any
sense of humanity does not make him too credible—except
at the very end. As the tyrant strikes him, the dying
Garcia professes anew his innocence, and accuses Piero of
having plotted the slaying of their brother, Diego.
Cosimo's situation resembles Philip's—he is left all
alone, his hands stained with blood; and he still has to
contend with the crafty Piero:

> Beloved Diego, do I lose thee! . . . Heav'ns!
> And in the lifeblood of another son
> I've bathed this dagger? . . . In the arms of death
> My consort lies: on my remaining son
> Frightful suspicions fall . . . O state! To whom
> Can I now turn? Alas! In whom confide?
>   [5.4]

Alfieri has succeeded again most effectively in isolating
the tyrant, in making him the real slave of power.

Rosmunda

The same level of content experimentation we found in
<u>Don Garcia</u> is pursued in <u>Rosmunda</u>, whose entire can-
vas was likewise Alfieri's invention. Although he was

very enthusiastic about this work, the author felt the
need to justify what he regarded as the poor choice of an
historical period. Once again, he regarded the high
Middle Ages as being deficient in the awe usually associ-
ated with ancient Greece or Rome. Rosmunda could not
induce that venerazione preventiva, or preconceived
veneration, necessary to the stature of a tragic character in the same measure as those characters who had
gained fame through the pages of Homer, Sophocles, or
Tacitus. True, she had been mentioned by Machiavelli,
who—Alfieri very poignantly wrote—lacked only one
prerequisite to be classified as a Tacitus: namely, that
the divided Italians become a single people (15). Yet it
was precisely because of the challenge of such shortcomings that Alfieri felt proud of his Rosmunda. He
owed only the characters' names to an obscure chapter of
medieval history—and they still came to life, thanks
entirely to his imagination.

Alfieri was aware of his position as a writer who had
heavily drawn upon works of other tragic authors. He was
convinced, however, that it was more difficult to appro-
priate well-known figures and events than to invent them
anew. Even if Alfieri's laborious efforts to forestall
possible criticism are somewhat bemusing, Rosmunda confirms that the master's skill in versification and struc-
turing rests securely on a well-established method of
composition. The four characters are all very different
indeed, each of them endowed with a highly individualized
intensity of feelings, with a convincing variation on the
overall polarization of love and hate. Yet, when all is
said and done, it is hard to single out a particularly
inspiring episode or a truly original psychological depiction. Even the final scene, in which Rosmunda stabs to
death Romilda—who is loved by both Rosmunda's husband
Alchimilde and by the noble Idovaldo—was borrowed from
Prévost's Memoires d'un homme de qualité, as Alfieri
himself pointed out (16).

A Slackening of Poetical Passion: *Mary Stuart*

In August, 1788, after conceiving and drafting the
prose version of The Conspiracy and Don Garcia in
Florence, Alfieri interrupted his work on the Prince and
Letters, and set down the first sketch of Maria Stuarda (Mary Stuart). The tragedy was first versified

in the months of March and May of 1779, while he was
still in Florence. The reworking was completed in Rome
in February, 1782 (17).

Alfieri asserted that this tragedy was the only one he
wished he had not written. He came to regard the well-
known story of Mary's death as not tragediabile, as not
suitable for tragedy, because Mary's death had been
ordered by Elizabeth, her natural rival and enemy. The
tension arising from a conflict among members of the same
family (according to Aristotle's principles, necessary
for a good tragedy) was therefore absent. Accordingly,
Alfieri chose to represent the death of Mary's husband,
Henry, and her falling victim to a false incrimination.

Even though the contrivance did not fully inspire him,
he pursued the theme and composed Mary Stuart for two
main reasons: first, it had been requested by the
Countess of Albany, to whom he could not refuse anything;
and second, it represented a challenge, it involved a
certain amount of pride. After writing eight tragedies
on subjects he had always found congenial, he wished to
try his hand at one that was not kindred to his taste,
and to verify whether he could make it acceptable a
forza d'arte, that is, through his poetical skill (18).
The statement points to Alfieri's constant preoccupation
with form and style; the perspective seems to anticipate
the writing of Merope, which he undertook in competition with Maffei's tragedy of the same name. His failure
with Mary Stuart serves to indicate that unless he had
a strongly inspiring story, his "art" alone could not
give life to it. Paradoxically, that was true even when
the plot possessed the inherent substance lent to it by
historical reality.

One personal note did filter into his tragedy nonetheless. It was a bitingly negative description of
Alfieri's personal "rival," the last heir of the House of
Stuart. Thus, Charles Edward Stuart, Pretender to the
throne of England, and the much despised husband of
Alfieri's beloved Countess of Albany, appears as totally
beneath contempt, unworthy even of the dignity of death
by the sword:

> O despicable race,
> Yes, thou wilt one day see thy end. O thou
> Last offshoot of it, will the sword destroy thee?
> No: not a hand is vile enough to deign
> To soil itself with blood like thine: thy life

Will pass in one long slothful sleep: while he
Who'll hold thy throne will not thy foeman be:
Thy battlefield will be the table: thou
In drunken revels wilt the memory drown
Of thy unmerited, untasted reign.

The dramatist later decided that such an open allusion
was not in the best of taste and had it omitted from the
printed text.   It remained in the manuscript, for Alfieri
felt that even if he did not want to "incur the stigma of
malignity, art required (!) that these verses should
remain" (19).

Return to the Ancients: *Octavia*

Ottavia (Octavia) was conceived in 1779, in
Florence, put into verse for the first time in 1781 in
Florence and Naples, and rewritten in a second versification in March, 1782, in Rome.   A very significant work in
Alfieri's conceptual evolution, it marks a return to
classical antiquity.   The author had been lamenting that
the "modern" settings of The Conspiracy, Don Garcia,
Rosmunda, and Mary Stuart had prevented his characters from wearing a wholly tragic aura.   Now he was
resolved to go back forever "among the Greeks, the
Romans, or other ancient peoples already made great (consecrated) by time" (20).
    Again it was in the pages of Tacitus that he found
what appeared to be an inspiring subject: the story of
Nero's wife, Octavia.   Her father, the Emperor Claudius,
had ill-advisedly given her in marriage to Nero, who
rejected her in favor of the ambitious Poppea, on the
pretext that she was unable to bear children.   In the
play Nero, fearing that exiled Octavia could somehow
incite the legions of Campania to rebel, recalls her to
Rome.   Unjustly accused of infidelity, she chooses to
take her own life rather than suffer an ignominious
death.   Along with Nero, Octavia, and Poppea, Seneca, the
philosopher and influential author of tragedies, and
Tigellinus, the corrupt courtier, take part in the
action.
    Two major components stand out in this drama: the new
emotional tonality Alfieri has given his heroine; and the
didactic poetics of the "useful," which Alfieri declared
to be the reason for the choice of a character such as

Nero. The author was convinced that by placing onstage the monstrous figure of the nefarious emperor, he could contribute to the fight against real tyrants like him (21). The exemplary value of the theater, as expressed in The Prince and Letters, is emphasized by Alfieri in his Parere or Opinion. He pointedly affirms that a tyrant can rid his country of all threats to power, except a good tragedy. He could forbid its representation, true, but he could never prevent the public from reading it and from remembering it after seeing it once. The very action of forbidding it would have a positive effect on its success, for it would stimulate an even greater interest in it. Even though a character like Nero could never move an audience to identify with him, he could nevertheless be a "useful" character according to the concept of the utility of literature, so relevant to the culture of the Enlightenment.

Nero provides another illustration of the constant state of fear a tyrant is condemned to live in. Since, however, he had to express a certain degree of greatness in order to be effective, the poet never depicted him as being too cowardly. His fear is brought out mostly through allusions made by others. When he is onstage, in his frequent reassurances to Poppea he even sounds strong and firm—though in a cruel, pitiless, and mad way.

Whereas Nero comes to signify the dark and evil side of human nature, Octavia stands for what is clear and noble in it. Once more, the feminine dimension of the character stands out; in Octavia's case, it is not Bianca's passionate femininity, nor the savage femininity of Clytemnestra, nor even Virginia's highly idealized womanhood. Alfieri seems to have forsaken in this tragedy any Plutarchian ideal of heroism, in favor of a more natural and less simplified representation of feelings and emotions. The two heroic characters in the play are incidental and purely functional, and besides, they never appear onstage. Octavia's alleged lover and her faithful lady-in-waiting, we learn indirectly, are prepared to suffer torture rather than accuse her of an adultery she has not committed.

Figures such as Isabella in Philip and Bianca in the Conspiracy are the forerunners of Octavia. Unlike them, however, she does not have the support of a loved one, of a Carlos or a Raymond. On the contrary, the element of love increases her tragedy for she is still strongly attached to her husband. The absurdity of this

love, which could appear as the weak point in the plot,
is actually only a weak point in human nature and becomes
a striking aspect of Alfieri's treatment of Octavia. The
poet is now exploring other psychological dimensions.
The victim stands out on the scene in all her frailty.
Her complexity shows a wealth of new ramifications in
Alfieri's sensibility; Octavia brings the author a step
closer to the central concept of Saul, where the oppressed and the oppressor become one and the same.

Octavia's first words reveal her fragile nature and
her elegiac acceptance of fate. As Nero cruelly reminds
her of why he has rejected her, she generously expresses
her wishes for a more fruitful union in terms that ring
with all the nostalgia of one who never was a mother:

> Thou in that didst well;
> Provided that another happier consort
> Than I, alas! e'er was, could render thee
> The joyful father of a num'rous offspring.
> I know thou hast not found, nor e'er wilt find,
> One who, as I love, loves thee.

[2.6]

Tears, silence, and sighs stand sharply in relief over
any other element. Essentially, they sum up Octavia's
character. They focus on a melancholy figure new to
Alfieri's theater. Octavia already displays the traits
of a Romantic persona. Did the new sensibility that
opened the door to the Romantic Age find some of its
roots in the Poetics of Aristotle? It was there that
he indicated "pity" as one of the means a tragic poet
must use to reach his public; and he connected with
"pity," as an essential factor in determining the validity of a tragedy, the concept of "pathos" (22). The character who moves within these constants falls victim to
passions that he himself cannot measure or understand,
and acts irrationally.

Octavia still loves Nero, no matter what his behavior.
Her suffering is increased because of this weakness, and
her character, and indeed the whole tragedy, like most of
Alfieri's works, comes to fit well within the Aristotelian parameters for tragic art.

Meanwhile, Octavia displays all the characteristics of
a Romantic heroine, with the consequence that, while the
behavior of the oppressed one is dictated by irrational
impulses, the tyrant's deportment seems to be ruled by

rationality. A paradox, incidentally, which history has
proven to be true time and time again. Octavia asks only
to be left alone with her sufferings:

> What have I ask'd of thee? What ask I now?
> A life obscure and solitary too,
> And <u>liberty to weep</u>.

[2.6]

She is seeking out, in short, a life-style that will
become almost mandatory for many respectable characters
of Romantic literature. Even though Alfieri's sensibility could not indulge solely in the representation of
souls like Octavia, he recognized their potential. His
best-known heroine, Myrrha, dwells within the same sphere
of "pity" and "pathos" inhabited by Octavia.

In spite of her wavering nature, Octavia reaches a
moment of perception and acts with strength by choosing a
voluntary death. But even in this final brave deed, she
who <u>feared</u> death is spared any show of bloody violence: she dies by poison.

Cesarotti, who was <u>Octavia</u>'s first critic, found the
scene insufficiently verisimilar (23). He did not regard
it as believable that Octavia would forcibly seize the
poison from Seneca. The author had some doubts himself
as he revised the final version in 1782, and not merely
with regard to style. In the first version Octavia was
simply given the fatal ring by Seneca; in the final
draft, not without an intentional ambiguity, Octavia is
able to obtain the ring more because of Seneca's weak
opposition than by her force. In both cases Seneca
realizes that death is the only solution to Octavia's
hopeless situation. Given the characters involved,
Alfieri regarded this solution as the most verisimilar
(24).

Octavia's emotional rhythm is maintained true to its
spirit until the end, so much so that in dying she still
speaks generously to Nero:

> The throne is thine: enjoy it:
> May peace be thine . . . Round thy ensanguined bed . . .
> I swear to thee . . . to never . . . never . . . come . . .
> A mournful spectre . . . to disturb . . . thy dreams

[5.5]

Alfieri insisted that this tragedy was very much a "daugh-

ter" of Tacitus, but there is no doubt that as a pathetic
elegy of Octavia's misdirected love, it was entirely the
poet's creation.

Merope

    In this period of intense labor, Merope acquires a
particular meaning. Alfieri had not yet given any of his
works to the press. His tragedies were known to a limited number of people; a select few who had heard him reading them, or had, perhaps, witnessed their rare private
representations. Yet he had acquired such a degree of
confidence in his art that he felt ready to challenge the
best the Italian theater of the eighteenth century had to
offer: Merope, by Scipione Maffei (1675-1755).
Alfieri knew Maffei's work quite well. In 1775 he had
expressed a less-than-flattering judgment on it. Alfieri
had been dismayed most of all by the language of the
dramatic Italian authors, Maffei included, and the lack
of (tragic) vigor in their diction. He was appalled that
a poetic vehicle that had been so "brief and ferocious"
in Dante could be rendered so "faded and castrated" by
modern authors (25). In 1782 a new reading of Maffei's
Merope sent him into fits of anger (26). How could
Italian readers and critics be so blind as to regard
Merope as an excellent play? The same subject could
lend itself, he felt, to a "simpler," "warmer," more
incalzante ("faster and more inexorable") treatment
(27).
    Thus, Alfieri's own Merope was born. It was written
with the purpose of establishing Alfieri's superiority
over Maffei, as well as affirming his supremacy over the
rest of Italian theater as a whole. Alfieri had earlier
rebelled against the type of poetry that had been born
out of the anti-baroque Arcadia. He had already detached
his style from a diction that appeared too languid to
him; he had divorced himself from exclusively melodious
verse. He had reformed tragedy in many of its structural
components. Now it was a question of making the public
aware of these novelties through a direct confrontation,
which really amounted to a rewriting of an acclaimed
masterpiece. Merope had been so successful since its
first appearance in 1713 that even the great Voltaire—as
we indicated earlier—had admired and imitated it. This
detail is of some relevance, for we should not exclude

the possibility that Alfieri also took the French writer as a rival to be surpassed. The crisis of maturity was coming to an end.

The plot of <u>Merope</u> fell nicely within the structure of tragic narrative. Polifonte (Polyphontes) had become king and tyrant of Messene by killing Cresfonte (Cresphontes) and his sons—all but Egisto (Aegisthus), who had been saved and taken away by Polidoro (Polydore). Fifteen years have gone by. Polyphontes now wants to marry Cresphontes' widow, Merope. She despises and hates him and lives only in the hope of seeing her son avenge his family. The son has returned, but as he approached the city, he was forced to fight and kill an unknown assailant, a youth of his own age. Arrested, he explains the occurrence and protests his innocence. Merope is peculiarly touched by the appearance of the young man, whom she fails to recognize. Her attraction to Aegisthus becomes a torment when she is led to believe that the slain youth was her son. Once convinced of this, she wants to kill Aegisthus, giving the play its moment of highest tension, for the audience knows that she would be slaying her own son. He is himself unaware that Merope is his mother. A reversal in the situation takes place when Polydore, who has meanwhile arrived in Messene, reveals the truth. Merope is desperate at the thought of her only son being in the hands of the tyrant. Polyphontes, however, promises to spare Aegisthus provided she consents to their marriage, which she is forced to do. When the ceremony is about to take place, Aegisthus seizes the priest's sacrificial ax and strikes Polyphontes down. The people of Messene, after a brief struggle with the tyrant's guards, recognize Aegisthus as their new king.

While this is not the place to go into a detailed and laborious comparison between the two works, it is the general consensus that Alfieri's play is indeed better than Maffei's. The treatment of the two respective slayings should suffice to demonstrate Alfieri's superior dramatic and poetic skill. While the mysterious youth killed in the beginning by Aegisthus is depicted by Maffei as a sort of wild robber, Alfieri makes him resemble Aegisthus himself, thus making Merope's mistaken identification more credible. In Alfieri's version the confrontation takes place not <u>on</u> the bridge leading to Messene, but—more plausibly—on a deserted path leading <u>to</u> the bridge. This glimpse of a solitary landscape

exemplifies the taste for the harsher aspects of nature,
which appears—in spite of its Dantesque flavor—as more
Romantic than Arcadian. The forbidding landscape is con-
sciously evoked by Aegisthus as he tells of his experience:

> I pursued
> A narrow and solitary path,
> Destined for humble travelers on foot,
> Which winds along Pamisus' shelving banks;
> Swiftly I trod this path, urged by desire
> To gain the city . . .
>
> [2.1]

An unknown figure approaches. He appears to be a bold
young man, an adversary worthy of Aegisthus:

> When lo! I saw a man advance to meet me,
> With eager gait, still swifter than my own:
> Onwards he came like one who fear'd pursuit;
> His mien was youthful; his demeanor bold,
> Imperative, and arrogant . . .
>
> [2.1]

The ensuing fight is determined by a question of puntiglio and precedence, or right of passage, as in a
later, famous scene in Manzoni's The Betrothed.
Maffei, instead, attributed the clash to a base intention
of robbery (28). In Alfieri's theater every character,
even those figures, like Aegisthus's aggressor, who do
not appear on the stage, bear the stamp of a would-be
superior nature. The weapon itself is nobler: rather
than Maffei's primitive club, Alfieri's character wields
a classic dagger. The very description of the fight has
a sensitivity for linear details that easily recalls a
single combat or athletic competition of epic descent.
    The effectiveness of the final scene, in the fifth
act, is heightened by having Polyphontes slain in full
sight of the spectators. In Maffei's Merope this
climactic action was reported by a secondary character,
according to a procedure that was, perhaps, more in keeping with classical tradition, but which lost—due to the
absence of a chorus—most of its dramatic impact.
Maffei's report of the action was furthermore encumbered
by useless details, some of which still reflected a certain baroque influence: the sacrificial bull that ran

amuck in the crowd; the agony of Adrastus, a guard, twitching on the ground in a pool of blood. Alfieri simplifies the design to a neoclassical clarity from beginning to end, in both action and style.

Without being great, Merope is, nevertheless, a well-polished play. The human vibration, which the author had attained with Octavia, is even better controlled. Merope is intended to magnify the anguish of a widowed mother on a grand scale. Alfieri successfully achieved his aim of making her a mother who is also a queen, with all the obligations pertaining to her rank. Aegisthus is a hero of liberty and vengeance, more poised than his predecessors. Even the tyrant, Polyphontes, appears much more restrained in his foxy endeavor. Every character thus seems to feel on a more human level. Their actions can be impetuous, as in the case of Aegisthus, but they are never frenzied. It is Alfieri's first tragedy that ends "well."

The author dedicated Merope to his mother. Without indulging in the intricacies of a Freudian analysis, we must briefly comment on the dénouement of this work in comparison with the preceding ones. In the very first play, Philip, it was the father-king who triumphed, ending, however, in a state of anguish. In Merope the situation is reversed: the son becomes king, taking the place once occupied by the father first, and then by the pretender to his mother's hand. The son enthrones himself, both politically and emotionally, at the apex of the pyramid of power. In this perspective, the resemblance of Aegisthus to the unknown assailant is more than just a plot expedient. It is as if Aegisthus, in killing his mirror image, had eliminated his old self, thus freeing his new persona and thereby making the fulfillment of his destiny possible. On the literal level, the killing of the stranger (as in the famous tragedy Oedipus) triggers the action. But the literal level is here in perfect accord with the symbolic one, with the subliminal identification of the poet with his characters. At the moment when he fully realized his stature as a writer of tragedies, Alfieri had also conquered a deeper understanding of himself.

Chapter Four
A New Sense of Humanity: *Saul* and *Myrrha*

Saul

Alfieri's path through his "crisis of maturity" was, creatively, a most fruitful one. It allowed him to externalize fluctuating spiritual and ideological issues in the poetical rendering of multifarious plots involving a wide variety of characters. Thus the possibilities of mankind for heroic strength, as well as all of its weaknesses and frailties, were analyzed and projected on the stage. The writing of Saul accentuated the ideological vacillation at the basis of the author's crisis. The dramatic contrast between strength and weakness, with all its spiritual and moral ramifications, is now centered within one grandiose character: Saul. All the potential characteristics of human nature are projected and magnified in his figure. Saul symbolizes, in a clearly Romantic fashion, the personal struggle everyone must engage in in order to affirm his own individuality. He also shows how to accept final defeat with courage and dignity.

It would be easy to say that the conceptual and artistic originality of Saul resides in the fact that Alfieri makes the figures of the tyrant and the victim merge and become one. All of Alfieri's tyrants are victimized by their own power, ambitions, and fears. What is new in Saul is that his character renders manifestly human the inner strife which leads him to folly. If, on the literal level, Saul's exalted state of mind is caused by divine punishment, in the play it is a metaphor for human weakness, but with no intention, on the part of the author, of condemning man's shortcomings. Alfieri's Plutarchian expectations have been modified; a new wisdom, which is also made of acceptance, is to be found at the core of his inspiration. The complexity of the situation, however, makes a solution hard to come by because the type of man he creates can never be brought down

without a titanic struggle. Thus the multiple motifs
that make up <u>Saul</u> alternate between the elegiac, the
melancholically lyrical, and the profoundly tragic. This
multiplicity of moods is mainly concentrated in the principal character, but it also finds expression in the
minor ones that gravitate within his orbit.

Alfieri was at the apogee of the creative season that
had seen his challenge to Maffei, when, inflamed by his
first reading of the Old Testament, he felt almost compelled to write <u>Saul</u> (1). The eminently poetic charge
of the imagery of the biblical texts impressed Alfieri
for its richness. He admired the writers of old for
their use of similes, their exaggeration of passions, and
their ability to confer verisimilitude on the impossible
by recourse to the supernatural. By contrast, he polemically blamed his own century for being too "rational" and
not at all "poetical." Since he deemed his contemporaries to be incapable of appreciating works reflecting
such high aesthetic principles, he restrained himself
from seeking further theatrical subjects in the Bible, as
he would have liked to do (2).

We can accept his justification, but it is obvious
that the poet had been particularly fascinated by the
titanic figure of Saul. The biblical king was a doomed
hero; forsaken by his God, he had been rendered impotent
to confront reality. That he struggled, nonetheless, is
what made him noble. His desperate stubbornness placed
him on the spiritual level that Romantic literature was
about to prescribe as the highest aspiration of the hero
(3). The biblical narrative structure was conceptually
suitable to Alfieri's conflicting interpretation of reality, and as a depiction of passionate, tragic humanity, it
provided a paradigm of greatness analogous to Plutarch's,
and to the Greek world as well.

The basic events of the drama are majestic and simple;
the writing is dramatically powerful. King Saul is
encamped in Gilboa, preparing to do battle against the
Philistines. David, who had been forced into exile by
the suspicions of his king, has secretly come back. He
meets his friend Jonathan, his adoring wife Michal, and
he makes peace with Saul. But Saul again falls prey to
his madness. Ahimelech, the priest whom the king suspects of plotting with David, is put to death with all of
his people. The ferocious act brings Saul more anguish,
not peace. David, to fulfill his destiny as the Anointed
of the Lord, leaves again. The Philistines attack and

destroy Saul's army, killing all his sons. Upon seeing
that all is lost, Saul turns his sword on himself.

Saul's action follows an internal, inescapable logic
and moves swiftly to its conclusion through a succession
of dramatic moments. Never before had all the familiar
elements of Alfierian tragedy been so well integrated and
so effectively woven together into an organic whole.
According to the rule we have observed, the main character does not make his entrance until the second act.
Through the three other personages of the tragedy, we
learn the antecedents of the action, but this is not a
mere technical expedient. The chief theme of the first
act is love. Saul's absence is dramatized by the love of
Michal and Jonathan for their father and for David, and
by the reciprocal love David bears the others; love is
the dominant motif in all their speeches.

The most touching figure is that of Michal. Her attitude and words express the feminine tenderness and frailty of the other heroines such as Isabella, Bianca, and
Octavia. Yet Michal moves alternately in melancholy,
elegiac, and tragic dimensions which, compounded in this
way, are new in Alfieri's poetry. Her novelty—like
Saul's—blooms in the humanity she exudes, with all its
fears, doubts, and hopes. Michal's polyphonic character
is the closest to Saul's in its composite conception, and
she reflects, modulates, and, at times, amplifies the
king's moods. As she brings them closer to us, she
acquires a function in the tragedy that she did not have
in the source: her biblical counterpart had hardly any
relief. The suffering, faithful wife in this drama is
entirely Alfieri's creation (4).

Jonathan, on the other hand, in his idolizing friendship for David, is a monochromatic, conventional character. So is David, immersed as he is in his sense of
righteousness, a feeling that is a consequence of his
knowledge that he is the Chosen of the Lord. In David's
and Jonathan's noble and stirring speeches a real tragic
tension seems to be present, but only momentarily. Nonetheless, the three secondary characters set the tone for
the action. They introduce a certain fluctuation of
contradictory emotions that will then reach its highest
pitch within Saul.

The play begins at night. The poetry of darkness,
which once more establishes the chromatic keynote at the
onset of the tragedy, is not a mere product of the
fashionable nocturnal poetry of the time. It authenti-

cally represents the projection of the inner feelings of
the characters. David's opening soliloquy circumscribes
topographically the wild and menacing setting of the
action: "These are Gilboa's mountains, / Now forming
Israel's camp, exposed in front / To the profane Philistines." Then it throws a dark flash on Saul's situation,
magnanimously but ominously ascribing his behavior to his
abandonment by God: "But Saul, I clearly see, in thought
is stricken; / His God abandons his perverted mind." The
soliloquy is obsessed by night, although the mind is projected toward the rising day, in which David sees a sign
of hope and of future great deeds: "Night, do thou soon
yield / Thy shades to the glad sun; for he today / The
witness of a gen'rous enterprise / Is destined to shine
forth." In David's anticipatory description the sun that
dominates is the sun that will shine for the Chosen of
the Lord; darkness and sunshine pattern a basic arche-
typal projection of good versus evil. Its later apparition in the scene of Michal, however, increases the dense
heaviness of night:

> Abohrr'd, eternal night, wilt thou ne'er vanish?
> But, doth the sun, indeed, for me arise
> The harbinger of joy? Unhappy I!
> Who in everlasting darkness live!
>
> [1.1]

Michal's words meaningfully sharpen the contrast established by David's exhortation to the rising sun.
Michal's night is qualified as "abhorred" and "eternal,"
thus acquiring a strong subjective connotation, which is
intensified by the statement that her life is indeed
immersed in the darkness of despair. The sun, anxiously
awaited by David, is the light of God which will shine
benevolently on him—but not so for Michal. The new day
will only bring her new suffering. Michal's accent of
melancholy and pain introduces one of the main motifs of
the work and preludes in somber anticipation the appearance of Saul, who enters the scene precisely at sunrise.

Of Past and Present

At the opening of the second act Saul's words are
solemn and, at the same time, humble. They reflect a
moment of lucidity. They express the melancholic acknowl-

edgment of man's limitations—no matter how great the
man. Once again, the temporal reference to the early
dawn is permeated with the character's mood: "This dawn
how beautiful! Today the sun / Arises not in bloody mantle wrapt; / He seems to promise a propitious day." The
cadence of the lines seems measured on the beat of Saul's
heart. However, over this moment of nostalgic interpretation of a new day weighs the allusion—ominous though
expressed in a negative form—to the "bloody mantle."
The very word "mantle" (ammanto) cannot but suggest a
close association with the regal garment of the same
name, thus establishing an anticipatory sense of contact
between "king" (Saul) and "bloody."

It is the dimension of the past that presses on Saul's
imagination: "O my past years! Where are ye now all
fled?" The universal theme of man's limitations takes on
a more personal connotation. Saul is growing old and
feels weak, in that his power, his authority, is slipping
from his grasp. His words ring with a sad and bitter
sense of inferiority and disappointment, with more than a
recognition of senescence, in his answer to Abner, who is
hypocritically trying to reassure him:

> O Abner, with what diff'rent eyes do youth
> And hoary age contemplate the events
> Of human life! When, with a well-knit arm,
> I grasp'd this ponderous and gnarled spear,
> Which now I scarce can wield; I ill conceived
> The possibility of self-mistrust . . .
>
> [2.1]

The core of Saul's drama is projected here in terms of a
biological polarization. In the reality of the tragedy
the two opposites, youth and old age, are personified in
the two contrasting characters, David and Saul himself.
Some critics legitimately point out that the torment of
old age is only one component of Saul's complex existential drama; nonetheless, especially on the literal level,
it remains a major metaphor, providing the basic dynamic
force of the play (5).

The flame that ignites Saul's tragic charge is a consequence of this polarization, and takes the guise of a
jealous rivalry toward the young and valiant David.
Saul's refusal to accept God's will isolates him from
everyone else and turns him into a titanic figure of solitude. His tortured soul is populated by a multitude of

vacillating impulses. If, in a lucid moment, he recognizes the reality of the situation:

> But I have now not only lost my youth . . .
> Ah! were but the invincible right hand
> Of God still with me! . . . or with me at least
> David, my champion lost!
>
> [2.1]

the very consciousness of his loss unveils an over-
whelming spiritual strength, for it takes an exceptional courage to admit one's insufficiency and to
accept total isolation. A further mesasure of Saul's
humanity is given by his profession of love for his
children: "Ah were I not a father, as I am / Alas!
too certainly, of much-loved children," he tells Abner
that he would already have sought death in battle. When
did one of Alfieri's tyrants speak of love before? The
poet has given his characters a new dimension, he has
opened new perspectives for them. Saul's intense self-
scrutiny, for instance, makes him one of the characters
closest to the heart of the poet. In announcing that he
is

> Ever impatient, fierce, disturb'd, and wrathful;
> I am a burden to myself and others;
> In peace I wish for war, in war for peace:
> Poison conceal'd I drink in ev'ry cup:
> In ev'ry friend I see an enemy; . . .
>
> [2.1]

he goes beyond objective description of a tortured state
of existence, applicable simply to the situation of the
character within the tragedy. The verbal texture of his
speech brings it extremely close to the referential connotations of the self-portrait of Alfieri contained in one
of his sonnets:

> Face paler than a throned king's in hue;
> Now hard and bitter, yielding now and mild;
> Malignant never, passionate always,
> With mind and heart in endless strife embroiled;
> Sad mostly, and then gayest of the gay.
> Achilles now, Thersites in his turn:
> Man, art thou great or vile? Die and thou'lt learn!

Like the character of Saul, Alfieri's own personality is
depicted as being basically composed of strongly contrasting elements, which are placed in sharp focus when personified in the antithetical figures of Achilles and
Thersites. In this sonnet the duality of human nature is
thrown into relief, as it is in the tragedy, where it
constitutes one of the main conceptual components.

Furthermore, when Alfieri writes of himself: "With
mind and heart in endless strife embroiled," he is revealing the inner strife that will be the common denominator of many literary heroes of the Romantic Age—but he
is also sketching in, in broad outline, the innermost
theme of Saul. The last line of the self-portrait,
furthermore, points to the ultimate test of all
men—death.

A key to Saul's alternating moods, his contrasting
assessment of reality, is offered by the king himself.
He says to Abner:

> And thou thyself, (too well thou know'st the
>   truth)
> Dost sometimes, as thou art, appear to me
> My kinsman, champion, and my real friend,
> The leader of my armies, the support
> Of my renown, and sometimes dost appear
> The interested minion of a court,
> Hostile, invidious, crafty, and a traitor . . .
>
> [2.1]

This antithetical structure splits Abner's personality
into two opposite halves. That is the deadly paradox of
Saul's condition: he has the capability of discerning
certain aspects of reality, but lacks the ability to pass
a proper judgment on them. This tragically ironic
situation is very skillfully compounded through Abner's
words. After Saul has painfully acknowledged the fact
that God has abandoned him, Abner retorts:

> Who to thee
> First dared to say, that God had cast thee off?
> The daring, turbulent, ambitious Samuel,
> The crafty, doting priest; whose palsying words
> His sycophantic worshippers repeat.
>
> [2.1]

This suggestion adds just the right amount of ambiguity

to the tragedy. Alfieri—who hardly acknowledged the
presence of God throughout his life—wrote in his
"opinion" on Saul that even if one does not accept
the concept of God's punishment, for the purpose of
the drama what really matters is that the king believes
it. The belief that he had fallen from divine favor
was enough to make him fall into his perturbed state of
mind (6).

Apparently, Alfieri considered the biblical God as
a conceptual equivalent of what "fate" represented in
the Greek world. However, in this tragedy Alfieri
depicts man as not so fatalistic; as no longer so ready
to accept God's will. Yet the forces he tries to overcome are so tremendous that he cannot but feel their
impelling presence. When both Jonathan and Michal—by
now aware of David's return to the camp—attempt to give
Saul new hope for victory, he does not conceal from them
the overpowering sense of impending doom he is experi-
encing. Saul's colossal physical build must have greatly inspired Alfieri, as it is evoked by powerful metaphor:

> What victory?
> What spirit comes? . . . Let us all weep, today
> That venerable oak, torn up, will show
> Its squalid roots, where heretofore it spread
> Its stately branches to the gales of Heaven.
> All, all is weeping, tempest, blood and death:
> Rend, rend your garments; scatter on your hair
> Polluting dust. Yes, this day is the last;
> To us, the final day.
>
> [2.2]

The finality of Saul's words has the ominous weight of
truth, and it contrasts greatly with the illusory hopes
of the others. Saul can see the approaching end, but he
can also see the dignity he can retain. Such a sense of
nobility is rendered by the image of the "venerable" oak
tree, still great even in its fall. Contrary to the
opinion of some critics, the personal pronoun us is not
simply a rhetorical pluralis maiestatis—it expresses
the common fate that awaits all those who are close to
the king (7). Like the wrath of fate, the wrath of God
can strike the innocent together with the guilty. From
the very beginning of the tragedy David had solemnly proclaimed such a possibility:

Ah, woe, if the Eternal sends His bolt
Of vengeance from the gaping firmament!
Thou know'st, that often in the fierce career
Of his retributory punishments,
He hath involved the guiltless with the guilty.

                                                    [1.2]

   The metaphors used in David's speech to render visually concrete this abstract concept were selected from the
field of vegetable imagery so typical of the Bible.   The
innocents are embodied here in "flow'rs, fruits, leaves,"
and the guilty in "foul and tainted plants." Subsequently, when dealing at closer range with the individual
character of Saul, the generic "tainted plant" has taken
the noble form of the oak tree. Still, when the oak is
felled, the branches and leaves must follow the trunk.
Saul's words are clear in the metaphor: when the king
falls, he will not fall alone.
   The tragedy preserves some ambiguity, even during
Saul's apparent acceptance of the returned David. The
king reproaches him paternally for his warrior's pride,
but is the king not actually speaking the truth? His
relation to reality, which at one moment expresses merely
the jealousy, envy, and fear of an old, weakening
monarch, at another moment seems to express the real
madness caused by divine punishment. Alfieri leaves the
question in suspense, and this provides the tragedy with
a continuous inner tension. Even if such fears were
unfounded, they were real enough in the mind of the old
Saul. The reconciliation of the second act will be a
short-lived one. By the third act (after some fast-paced
scenes with the participation of the secondary characters
only) Saul is again the victim of his fears. To his
eyes, the sun appears surrounded by a "fatal wreath of
blood," the air resounds with the singing of "ill-omened
birds." When he realizes that David's sword is the one
that belonged to Goliath, the precious trophy that has
been hung in the tabernacle in Nob, his suspicions seem
confirmed. Upon hearing that Ahimelech, the priest, has
given it to David, he explodes in all his fury. He feels
stripped of everything: "the sun, my kingdom, / My
children and my pow'r of thought, all, all / Are taken
from me." He stands alone.
   In this play, more than in any other, Alfieri illustrates the fact that the irony of destiny is such that
what gives one peace of mind and joy, is often the same
agent—whatever it may be—that also gives pain and

sorrow. The same David, who is literally the cause of
Saul's suffering, succeeds in calming him with his singing, as he used to do in the past (8). Yet David's charm
does not provide a permanent solution, as his boasts of
military prowess provoke new fits of anger in the king,
and Michal begs her husband to flee.

By the fourth act Saul's figure has grown to titanic
stature, and he easily dominates the scene. As if having
reached the ultimate source of the contrasting forces
that besiege him, he seems to recognize God's inscrutable
will: "Tremendous hand, I now begin to know thee"--yet
he cannot accept it because he feels free from any guilt.
In the ambiguous dimension of Saul's surrogate political
interpretation of his role, David again becomes the "instrument of sacerdotal malice"; not the Chosen of the
Lord. Saul considers himself to be unjustly punished.
For him, not killing the conquered Agag had been an act
of mercy. Who then is to blame? Not God, but the
priests:

> . . . cruel priests, revengeful, thirsty ever
> For human blood? To Samuel did it seem
> A crime unpardonable that I slew not
> The King of Amalek, with arms in hand,
> Taken in flight; a mighty king, a warrior,
> Of ardent gen'rous temper, and profuse
> Of his own life-blood in his people's service.
> Unhappy king! dragg'd in my presence, he
> Came manacled: yet he preserved, though vanquish'd
> A noble pride . . .

[4.4]

Saul's assessment of King Agag is interestingly subjective. The "noble pride" of the vanquished monarch resembles closely Saul's own. He is not punished for a
merciful act, but for not following those rules of tribal
ethics that demand the elimination, when possible, of all
powerful enemies. The priests are the precise emblems of
such unyielding ethics. Saul's tirade against the priest
class—whom he defines as a "selfish, cruel, and malig-
nant tribe"—must not be interpreted as empty rhetoric,
but as an expression of Alfieri's polemical attitude
toward the Church. The poet has effectively combined
political, religious, and biological (Saul's old age)
elements to give life to a most compellingly complex
character and situation (9).

On the other hand, the priest, Ahimelech, has some

strong, prophetic accents of his own. Transcending the
particularity of the situation, in his answer to Saul he
entreats the king to examine himself and to realize that
he is "but a crown'd heap of dust." His statement is as
subjective as any pronounced by Saul. It acquires a personal ring as it voices the biblical assessment of the
status of mankind: an assessment reached by Alfieri,
too, in his maturity. The realization of the common
boundaries that limit man's action in life was not to be
found in Alfieri's previous works.

Saul remains deaf to Ahimelech's words. Rather than
abating his pride, the priest's pronouncement spurs him
to action. He rescinds David's orders to the troops to
engage battle in the afternoon—for he regards it as a
reflection on his declining strength—then discharges his
fury against the priests. Nob is to be destroyed; "ser-
vants, and cattle, mothers, houses, babes, / And to the
desolating winds disperse / All the flagitious race."
The poet adheres almost verbatim to the biblical text.
He has given us, however, a fascinating interpretation of
the psychological process that led Saul to this last display of power.

Alfieri's vision of mankind, as construed in the
king's psychological rapport with religious beliefs,
prompts Saul's exclamation: "Thy priests may now /
Exclaim with truth: There is a Saul!" Far from the
mere expression of a madman, these words exemplify Saul's
ultimate effort to affirm his individual will above any
other. As a mythological titan, he wants to substitute
his own tangible presence—his concrete power—for the
power of an abstract superior being. The cry, "There is
a Saul," is the answer to Ahimelech's menacing allusion
to God; it is the cry of man's rebellion against outside
forces that seem determined to crush him. Of course, the
rebellious affirmation of individuality isolates him from
society. At the end of the fourth act Saul has rejected
all cautionary suggestions from Jonathan and Michal and
is again left to himself: "Myself alone, / (Unhappy
king!) myself alone I dread not."

"The Howling of the Haughty Victors"

The brief and intense fifth act opens with the elegiac
interlude of Michal's separation from David. Shortly
thereafter Saul appears on the scene, the victim of

remorseful hallucinations, but still a grandiose, kingly
presence. We had heard almost the same words ("Incensed,
tremendous shade, oh go thy way!") in Aegisthus's mouth;
the analogy does not detract from the originality of
Alfieri's creation. It confirms that his psychological
penetration gave him the capability of transforming the
deepest aspects of our subconscious into a universal pattern of poetical expression. The ghost haunting Saul's
mind is first Samuel, then Ahimelech, and then his children. Saul describes them to the distressed Michal in a
crescendo of terror and dismay. Only the clamor of the
intervening battle seems to bring the king's mind back to
reality—the Philistines have anticipated Saul's orders
and are now launching a surprise attack in the pre-dawn
darkness.

Everything crumbles around the monumental figure of
the old monarch. The fleeing Abner announces the victory
of the enemy and the slaying of the king's sons. It is
the end of the house of Saul, of his "ill-starr'd pro-
geny!" Precisely in these catastrophic final moments
Alfieri's Saul attains the summit of his regal dignity.
Torn with pain, he uses his authority—"and I yet am
king"—to save his daughter by having her removed from
his side. His last command is thus an order aimed at
saving life, not destroying it. Michal's anguish moves
him, yet he does not break down, for "a conquer'd king
should never weep." The Plutarchian hero emerges again
in Alfieri's imagination, but how much richer in humanity
than his predecessors.

The Philistines are approaching in all their fury, but
the king will not give them the opportunity to slay him.
Abandoned by all, he still has his sword:

> But, thou remain'st to me. O sword: now come,
> My faithful servant in extremity.
> Hark, hark! The howling of the haughty victors:
> The flashing of their burning torches glares
> Before my eyes already, and I see
> Their swords by the thousands . . . O thou vile
> Philistia,
> Me thou shalt find, but like a king . . . here . . .
> dead!

[5.5]

Saul does indeed die solemnly, but like a man who is master of his fate, who can determine the ultimate act of

his life. This transference of power from God to himself
is forcefully symbolized by the very weapon he employs,
the sword. Abner's prophecy of God's vengeance had taken
the biblical image of the "pitiless, retributory sword"
as unsheathed by "death's dreadful angel." Neither the
sword of divine justice, nor the blades of the Philistines could bring Saul down. Only his own weapon, as an
extension of his will, could terminate his tempestuous
life (10). Thus dies the last great personage of
Alfieri's theater.

A Brief Interlude: *Agis* and *Sophonisba*

Saul had been Alfieri's fourteenth tragedy. At that
point, he had reached—he felt—the maximum number of
works he wanted to write. He had, in fact, composed two
more than he had intended (11). His satisfaction was
immense, for he had, in a period of nine months, put into
verse seven tragedies; invented two new ones; and dictated, with corrections, all fourteen of those so far
written. He was also pleased with the results of his
"squirming test"—having read most of them on different
occasions to mixed groups of people, he was happy to see
that none of his listeners had been squirming in his
chair! This was an absolute proof of interest and appre-
ciation of his work (12). Alfieri's self-irony and sense
of humor are evident here, but they hardly conceal the
author's pride.

The happiness and satisfaction of that Roman period,
however, were to be brought abruptly to an end. To avoid
any possibility of scandal and papal interference, he
decided to leave Rome and his beloved Countess of Albany.
An interlude of approximately two years of gloom ensued.
In Siena he kept very busy caring for the first edition
of his works; he traveled widely also, writing in the
meanwhile a profusion of sonnets and letters. In 1784,
after being reunited with the Countess at Colmar, in
Alsace, he found the inspiration to conceive three new
tragedies: Agide (Agis), Sofonisba (Sophonisba),
and Mirra (Myrrha). Two more years had to pass, however, before he could complete these new works, among
which Myrrha was to be his last great tragic creation.

The joy of the brief reunion with his beloved one had
been embittered by the news of his friend Pietro Gori-
Gandellini's death. A new separation from the Countess

distracted him even further from his work. Only the reading of Pliny the Younger's Panegyric on Trajan the following year spurred him to write again. It was a new challenge, for he felt that such a work was unworthy of its author, and he persuaded himself to compose his own.

This enterprise cleared his mind of "many sorrows" and opened a new phase of creative activity. He corrected and finished the first book of The Prince and Letters. Then, again in Colmar, in December, 1785, came the writing out of the three new tragedies. The versification came the following summer. In the meanwhile he went on with the Prince; he wrote the Dialogo della virtù sconosciuta (Dialogue on Unrecognized Virtue); composed and partially put into verse Abele, a new genre of work which he dubbed a "tramelogedy" (a combination tragedy and "melodrama"); and finally, in emulation of Voltaire, conceived two other tragedies: Bruto Primo (The First Brutus) and Bruto Secondo (The Second Brutus).

A critical moment in his life had produced no definite spiritual and ideological solution. If anything, his attitude, in the face of irreconcilable divergences of human life, had become even more polarized in its negative extremes. During his brief reunion with the Countess his melancholy mood had been made more profound, as we saw, by the death of Gori-Gandellini. He wrote then to Mario Bianchi and Teresa Mocenni, their common friends, in Siena, that he felt "satiated by all things worldly," and his will to survive was determined only by his love for the Countess (13). Even in his emotional polarization a modicum of acceptance toned down his rebellious attitude. All three of the new tragedies reflect this change; their common denominator goes beyond the similarity of their typical external structure, and a new bend is manifest in the main characters of the tragic action.

The action is in fact precipitated, within the economy of the play, by the fact that their drama is mostly conditioned by forces existing within the characters themselves and only partially by concrete outside factors. In Myrrha the woman's sufferings find their roots entirely within her tormented soul.

Agis and Sophonisba were both regarded as mediocre works by their author. For the character of Agis, Alfieri went back to Plutarch. Though he also defined the play as his fourth tragedy of liberty, are we really back in the same heroic dimension as Virginia,

Timoleon, and The Conspiracy of the Pazzi (14)? Hardly. We are closer to and, at the same time, immensely
distant from, that of Saul. Whereas Saul was an aging
monarch, fearful of losing his power and his authority,
Agis is a very young king who idealistically wishes to
reform the state by reapportioning wealth and property to
all people in the same measure. This could be accomplished, he reasons, by reestablishing, in Sparta,
Lycurgus's ancient laws. Thus, while the typical hero of
liberty struggles for political freedom, Agis's aspiration is to redeem injustice and to give something to the
people through the use of his own authority, not by
rebellion. The dramatic tension of the play is provided
by the opposition of Leonidas, co-ruler of the State, who
is backed by Sparta's powerful oligarchy. There are no
obscure forces of fate to battle, nor is the inexorable
vengeance of God to be feared. Instead, one man's will
contrasts with sharply defined political interests.

Even after Leonidas has succeeded in imprisoning Agis,
the play is devoid of any imprecations against destiny,
or of any titanic acts of rebellion. Agis is ready to
face death with calm and dignity, his only wish being
that his life not be given uselessly. Even though
Alfieri does not quite succeed in making his character
leap fully into existence, the pathos that is in his
soul surfaces sporadically from the depths of the long,
rhetorical speeches that abound in the play.

The fourth act is, in this respect, a focal point.
The figure of Agis becomes imposing, in spite of his
youth, through the somber mode in which he affirms his
innocence and his readiness to die for Sparta. How different, however, is the tone from Saul's hammering sen-
tences:

> . . . to the prison willingly I went,
> And willingly in judgment I appear:
> Whate'er that judgment is, I fear it not.
> I wish'd it, and exult in its conclusion;
> And I exult in making myself heard.

[4.3]

If the changes he had envisioned for Sparta's society
require that his blood be spilled, he is anxious for it:

> Now is the time,
> Trust to my words, mature for such a change:

Heav'n does not will that I should witness it;
But it decrees its advent: Agis's blood
Is indispensable to hasten it,
And Agis yields that blood. I pity feel
For you, not for myself: these are the words
Of one whose only object is to die,
And to the tomb conveys no other wish,
Except to save his country.

[4.3]

The Plutarchian hero, ready to sacrifice his life for
his country, is still with us, but he is of an entirely
different breed. His words anticipate the patriotic
creed of the young Italians who will offer their lives
for the independence of their country in the following
century. As the rhetorical vein seems to overpower the
poetical one, Alfieri's lines acquire an almost purely
political connotation.

This tragedy's dedicatory letter and the subsequent
"opinion" of the author betray a strong polemical posture. Dedicated ironically to the late Charles the First
of England, Agis is an example of conduct diametrically
opposed to that of the king. Whereas Agis's death had
been caused by his sincere desire to reestablish equality
and liberty, Charles's was determined by his attempt to
"violate all limits" of authority, while procuring his
own "private good" (15). Agis's design had been "generous and sublime," Charles's had been vile and "common to
the herd of monarchs." Unfortunately, added Alfieri,
there had been only one Agis, while there had been many
Charleses.

The poet's words were harsh and direct and were clearly intended as an ethical condemnation of contemporary
politics. The author's "opinion" assumes even more
pronounced patriotic overtones. Alfieri believed that
Agis's actions, against the background of current morality, could be regarded as those of a madman. Only by
restoring true values, could his deeds be properly regarded as "sublime." Since in Italy "the plant of man"
(la pianta uomo)—as he affirmed in a metaphor that was
to become proverbial in Italian literature—grows more
robust than anywhere else, Alfieri hoped that his own
countrymen could be inspired to perform just such a reno-
vation (16).

Nevertheless, precisely because of the patriotic
rhetoric, the edifying character of Agis lacks the con-

vincing power of his predecessors. Even the final scene
of the suicide (a double one, for Agis's mother follows
her son's example) is conducted so coldly and flatly that
if fails to move us.

Agis's strong vis polemica enlivens and animates
the play to a certain extent; the machinery of Sophonisba, instead, relies entirely on the grandiosity of its
historical backdrop. The Second Punic War between Rome
and Carthage—the action is set in 203 B.C.—is the con-
spicuous contrivance Alfieri uses to validate the story
of Asdrubal's daughter, Sophonisba, who is torn apart by
her hatred for Rome and her love for the Numidian king,
Massinissa.

Massinissa is compelled, in the end, to offer the
woman he loves a bowl of poison. Such an act was regarded by Alfieri as being eminently adapted to produce that
sense of pity he deemed essential to a tragic occurrence.
The illustrious names of Scipio Africanus, Sophonisba,
and Massinissa would do the rest, but somehow the poet
could not attain the intensity of action he desired. He
seemed to have reached such a level of stoic acceptance
of life that it prevented him from injecting into his
characters the psychological complexity and the emotional
pitch typical of his previous work. The dramatic tension
is dissolved rather than enhanced by the quality of noble
abnegation common to all the characters. The very magnanimity of Scipio greatly diminishes the play of contrasting forces that one had come to expect in Alfieri's
theater.

Extreme Pessimism: *Myrrha*

Alfieri reaches his deepest level of inward expression
in the treatment of the existential anguish of the ill-
fated Myrrha, as her sorrows come entirely from within.
In essence, the action of the play is determined by her
struggle to overcome the obscure passion that subjugates
her. Reminiscent of Clytemnestra's inner conflict,
Myrrha's external structure is very simple and, due to
its lack of a political dimension, almost bourgeois in
its family-life setting.

Myrrha is the young daughter of Cinyras, king of
Cyprus, and his wife Cecris. She is the promised bride
of the handsome Pereus, son of the king of Epirus. In
spite of the love everyone feels toward her—including

her old nurse Eurycleia—she appears to become more and
more tormented by the unexplainable state of gloom and
despair.

Intuitively, Alfieri had known all along that the most
formidable adversary anyone has to face is himself.
While this was apparent in all of his preceding works, in
Myrrha he seems to have wanted to penetrate directly to
the core of such a concept by eliminating as much as
possible any outside interference. The story of Myrrha's
incestuous passion for her father was a well-known one.
Alfieri was aware of the scabrousness of the subject, yet
he had been so moved by Ovid's rendition of the young
woman's suffering, he felt he could write a well-grounded
tragedy by concentrating on that theme (17). In Ovid's
version [Metamorphoses, Book X, V] Myrrha's passion is
consummated by the stratagem of a nocturnal disguise,
after which she escapes to a distant land and is trans-
muted into the sensuous myrrh tree. Alfieri does not
allow the character to slip that far. In fact, the
thought of satisfying her lustful desire does not even
enter her mind. The moment she is brought to confess her
awful secret, she stabs herself. Her torment ends with
her life. Furthermore, Alfieri's intention was that the
spectator should not be aware of the origin or of the
cause of Myrrha's suffering until the climactic dénouement. Given such a device, making her an intriguing
tragic figure was not an easy task for the author to
carry into effect. That it works is due entirely to his
consummate skill. Alfieri succeeds in compelling us to
become so engrossed with Myrrha's behavior that we forget
what causes it. The tragedian's art is now so accomplished that, almost paradoxically, he can create an
eventful action where apparently there would be none.

Myrrha is yet another play of love; all the drama's
characters are moved by love. The goddess Venus is the
sixth invisible participant; her ever-present force dominates the action. The tension stems from the fact that
Myrrha's love is a misdirected one. By permitting a growing awareness of its incestuous twist, the obsessively
developed theme of conscience sustains and amplifies the
tension. Without the component of guilt, the situation
would have been so lacking in tension as to become banal.
In order to give a universal meaning to his heroine's
strife, the poet subtly weaves the role of the goddess of
love into the drama.

According to the ancient fable, Myrrha's passion had

been kindled by Venus's desire for revenge, since Cecris
had asserted that her daughter's beauty was superior to
that of the goddess. Far from emphasizing the motif of
individual revenge, Alfieri sharpens the paradoxical
aspect of Myrrha's passion. He knew only too well how
the sentiment of love, which he regarded as the noblest
of sentiments, could cause such a fatal torment as to
turn love for another into hate for oneself. In the
abnormal, extreme case of Myrrha the theme found a most
exemplary illustration.

No matter how much this drama may represent a particular and idiosyncratic conceptualization of passion, the
poet did succeed in creating an enduring figure of brooding melancholy and sorrow. By the side of that ultimate
model of the masculine hero embodied by Saul, Myrrha—in
the scheme of Alfieri's vision of human nature—shines as
the quintessential feminine character. The poet reached
this peak after a long process of evolving interpretive
portrayals of women. Isabella, Bianca, and Octavia represent so many modes of awareness of their feminine nature.
Even the rather opaque Sophonisba could not restrain a
burst of inner strength:

> Believe my words: although I do not weep,
> I feel my bosom rack'd with agony:
> I am a woman: nor make I parade
> Of virile courage: but there doth remain
> No path for me to take, save that of death.
> [Sophonisba, 5.5]

"I am a woman." Even though Myrrha does not pronounce
these very words, they seem to echo throughout her drama.
Alfieri's theater is entirely populated by captivating
feminine figures. How far these women are from the conventional representation of women in eighteenth-century
literature! How much more dense is their psychological
and emotional life; how much more willful their presence!

The image of Myrrha, as seen through her mother's
description at the beginning of the play, remains unforgettable, conditioning our reaction to every one of her
subsequent attitudes:

> It is true, that I
> For a long time have seen the lustre languish
> Of her rare beauty: obstinate and mute,
> A mortal melancholy dims in her

That fascinating look: and could she weep! . . .
But when with me, she's silent: and her eyes
With tears are pregnant, though forever dry.

[1.1]

The last paradoxical detail of the eyes brimming with
tears, but dry, is most effective in visually synthe-
sizing both Myrrha's inner strife, and the strength she
must draw upon to control it.   Clearly it was not
Alfieri's intention to represent his heroine in too sentimental a light.   He did not want her cast in a weaker
mold, nor did he intend to compose a tragédie larmoy-
ante in the tearful style of his French contemporaries.
He wanted a tragedy that, in spite of its touching (and
touchy) subject, could retain the dignity of his other
creations.

In the first act Myrrha is seen entirely through the
eyes of others.   However, the overall situation remains
enveloped in a shroud of mystery.   In the absence of any
discernible external motive for her distress Myrrha's
state of being cannot be attributed to any plausible
cause.   The other characters can only express their dedication to her and the dismay they experience in seeing
her radiant beauty obfuscated by unknown sorrows.   A
strong sense of tragic irony runs through the play,
finding its roots precisely in the affection that binds
the participants to the action.   Even the sarcasm of fate
is accentuated by Cinyras's expression of love for his
daughter.

Cinyras's attitude, furthermore, is a measure of his
distance from Alfieri's other kings (or tyrants) as the
end-product of a process of total "humanization."   If the
poet had already injected a strong element of love in the
figure of Saul, in creating Myrrha's Cinyras he goes
much further, and he will have Cinyras say:

Nature made me a father; chance, a king.
Those which are deem'd by others of my rank,
Reasons of state, to which they are accustom'd
To make all natural affections yield,
In my paternal bosom would not weigh
Against one single sigh of my dear daughter.

[1.3]

Cinyras's statement sounds like an indictment of all the
preceding monarchs—"others of my rank"—in Alfieri's

theater. To those sovereigns (like Philip, the first
king-father we encountered) who let "reasons of state"
take precedence over their human affections, Cinyras's
formula could be applied in reverse, for he acted as if
nature had made him a king, while only chance had
made him a father.

The shift in Alfieri's conception is not independent
of the changing cultural climate: Myrrha herself is a
character who has undergone the evolution from the Age of
Enlightenment to that of Romanticism. Who more than
Myrrha foreshadows the typical heroine of Romantic literature? How close Myrrha was to the poet, to his surging
"Romantic" moodiness, is apparent throughout the play;
one particular moment can be taken as most symptomatic of
the new subjective trend of expression. When Myrrha
first appears onstage (in the second act), she is gently
confronted by her betrothed, Pereus. To his concerned
questioning as to her apparent distress on the vigil of
their nuptials, she returns a dreamy picture of an inner
dimension of experience unthinkable in a classical context:

> . . . but pensiveness
> Is oft a second nature; ill could one
> Who feels its potent sway, explain the cause:
> And often an officious questioning,
> Instead of making manifest the cause,
> Redoubles the effect.
>
> [2.2]

These verses suggest that the poet is identifying with
his character. In fact, her statements acquire an extremely subjective connotation and seem to be a projection of his feeling and convictions. Myrrha is depicted
as being caught between knowing the cause of her melancholy and refusing to admit it, even to herself; yet in
the end her awareness prevails.

It should be pointed out that Charles Lloyd's English
version narrows the more general significance of the
original, by omitting to translate the emphatic plural
object pronoun noi ("us") in the last sentence uttered
by Myrra above. As in a similar case in Saul, the pronoun is not to be interpreted as a pluralis maiestatis,
but as the sign of collectivizing function. Its compre-
hensive value, moreover, is wider than in Saul, where
the circle of collectivity was only broad enough to

include the king's family. In this episode of Myrrha
it is intended to encompass all kindred spirits; all
those individuals stricken with that malaise which in the
literature of Romanticism will be known as the mal du
siècle. That Alfieri regarded himself as belonging to
such a melancholic breed is apparent from the many allusions scattered throughout his writings, especially in
his letters and autobiography.

Myrrha's drama emphasizes once more the loneliness of
the individual who is condemned by the power of passion
to feel alienated from society. The rules of the collectivity have been violated, and the outcast suffers the
most dire consequences:

> I am abandon'd by the gods; my breast
> Is open to the onslaught of the Furies;
> There they alone authority possess,
> And residence.
>
> [2.4]

Those who are close to Myrrha suspect correctly that the
force of love causes her present torment, but they cannot
divine for whom, or for what. Their constant attentions
and their sorrow contribute to exacerbating her own
grief. She feels "a burden to myself, a curse to
others," a typical predicament in which all of Alfieri's
personages seem to fall. They all find themselves caged
in, as if imprisoned in a situation that precludes any
possible way of escape but one: death. The tone of
Myrrha's words reflects, at the highest level of intensity, the same intuition of an existential tragedy, which
is, however, central to all of Alfieri's works. The
images describing her "insufferable, fierce vicissitude"
show her quivering in an ordeal of antithesis (food-
poison, sleep-wakefulness, dream-nightmare, day-night,
peace-restlessness, comfort-death), which moves fitfully
but relentlessly toward the negative release of annihil-
ation:

> My rare and little food to me is poison:
> Sleep everlastingly forsakes my pillow;
> Or dreams, with horrid images of death,
> Give greater martyrdom than sleepless nights:
> I do not find, throughout the day or night,
> A moment's peace, repose, or resting place.
> Yet nothing in the shape of human comfort

Do I presume to covet; death I deem,
Expect, solicit, as my only cure.

[3.2]

These lines express the deepest core of Alfieri's tormented vision of life, as he projects it onto his characters.   This spiritual, intellectual, and emotional
proximity allows us to perceive how the poet, for all the
gallery of heroes and heroines he placed upon the stage,
created, in reality, only one personage.   The same arche-
typal soul successively traverses, as he himself did, one
crucial existential crisis after another.
    By the end of the tragedy, the illusion of love, that
had characterized the opening of the action, is completely demolished.   Myrrha's obscure illness has spilled out
and has contaminated all those around her.   Even her
suicide—as well as that of Perseus—is completely devoid
of redeeming ritualistic value.   Deprived of political
overtones as it is, the self-slaughter is not an enno-
bling gesture, but rather an act intended to annihilate a
reality.   Myrrha dies in complete disgrace.   She has had
to confess her passion to her father; this has also meant
acknowledging it fully to herself.   Had it been possible
for her to take her secret with her to the grave, she
could have at least remained innocent in the others' eyes
and have been preserved guiltless in their memory; not
even this last comfort was allowed her.   Myrrha's last
words to her old nurse—for her parents have abandoned
her in horror—will be words of reproach for not having
let her die sooner:

    When I ask'd . . .
I . . . of thee . . . thou, . . . O Euricleia,
    . . . then
Shouldest . . . have given . . . to my hands
    . . . the sword:
I had died . . . guiltless; . . . guilty . . .
    now . . . I die.

[5.4]

    Myrrha and Saul are commonly considered Alfieri's
masterpieces.   They could also be regarded as masterpieces that complement each other.   While Alfieri put
much of himself into all of his characters, his most
profound point of contact with them is, however, to be
identified with these two great creations.   In the Saul

and <u>Myrrha</u> diptych, his <u>animus</u> and <u>anima</u>—the heroic masculine projection and its feminine counterpart —merge together to form an organic whole. Possibly this supreme achievement prevented Alfieri from giving life to any other such personages afterwards, except for one in his masterful autobiography—himself.

Chapter Five
The Realization of the Self

A Utopian Vision

Prior to composing the first draft of the first part of his autobiography (1790), Alfieri brought to completion a series of other literary enterprises (1). Though they encompass a vastly heterogeneous production, these works are characterized by a common mental attitude that tends more and more toward a return to autobiography. Alfieri's very first literary experiments included, in fact, writings of an autobiographical nature. The Giornali (Journals), never published, written between 1774 and 1777, partially in French, demonstrate that the autobiographical impulse precedes even his tragic production (2). Although, in a wider sense, all of Alfieri's works are autobiographical, yet the prose essays completed between 1786 and 1790 seem exceptional among his works for their pronounced personal accent. (It goes without saying that the Rime [Poems] in their lyricism constitute a kind of spiritual diary, even those devoted to political subjects, which bears the imprint of a rhetorical and didactic structure.) Derived from the reading of Italian authors and French "philosophes," these writings constitute the external manifestations of the different moments of an inner individual process. They are animated by the same will to clarify, illustrate, even demonstrate the validity and sincerity of a chosen line of conduct. They all integrate with each other to this end.

The genesis of On Tyranny is to be identified mainly with the reading of Titus Livy, Machiavelli's Storie Fiorentine (Florentine Histories), and Plutarch's Lives; however, in spite of its scientifically objective overall structure, the essay is a very personal expression. In The Prince and Letters it seems clear that the ideal figure of the man of letters is patterned on Alfieri's own projection of himself and of his own aspirations. In the Dialogue of Unrecognized Virtue the author appears as one of the two interlocutors. In the Panegyric of Pliny Alfieri substitutes himself for

Pliny. In the two Brutuses the essential concepts developed in the essay are brought to life in the persons of these famous heroes of liberty. Finally, the Opinions Alfieri wrote on each of his tragedies are necessarily expressed in the first person; but this is more than a grammatical device, it is a basic stylistic dimension which confronts the reader—as in the numerous letters to his friends—with the same narrating "I" as in the Vita.

In our discussion of Alfieri's poetics we stressed that On Tyranny and The Prince and Letters were aimed at clarifying literary issues also. Each of these works was preceded by a sonnet. In the case of the first treatise the poem was a bitter and resentful statement intended to defuse any possible criticism and condemnation of the author's works and character. Those who might accuse him of writing too much, too harshly, and too exclusively against tyrants were defiantly assured that he would never turn aside his will or his art from such a "sublime" purpose. It was his conviction that his words would not be scattered on the wind if, in the future, men worthy to be called free should be born with their aspirations aimed toward Liberty as an integral part of their lives (3). While this treatise was dedicated to liberty, Alfieri dedicated The Prince and Letters—in a somewhat sarcastic vein—to "those Princes who do not protect literary endeavors."

The sonnet that precedes The Prince, however, displays an equally ironic but more benign attitude. The tone is subdued, dream-like. A visionary convention (pareami in sogno, "it appeared to me as in a dream") frames it. In his imagination the poet sees himself transported to the top of Mount Parnassus, among the Muses. The Muses declare that they descend not from Jupiter, but from Liberty, and they enjoin him to go and proclaim this truth unabashedly; possibly in the future it may stir those prostrated in slavery to awaken toward freedom (4).

In the first chapter of the present work we saw the relevance that these two treatises had to the saturation of Alfieri's tragic production with his moral convictions. The Dialogue and the Panegyric also constitute an integral part of that whole.

The Dialogue is an intriguing essay, even in its external structure. After a work that espouses, albeit in a poetical form, Machiavelli's predilection for effec-

tive reality, Alfieri now turns to a work of a more
imaginative nature. The classical form of the dialogue
is further enriched by the addition of a pre-Romantic
nocturnal and spectral dimension, possibly a reflection
of the taste for the "graveyard" poetry that was becoming
fashionable at the time. The exchange takes place between the author and the ghost of his friend Francesco
Gori-Gandellini. Within this fanciful framework, however, the classical dimension prevails. The "virtue" of
the title refers to his friend's virtue, which would pass
unrecognized unless the poet himself spoke about it (5).
Francesco becomes the author's true spokesman. In
response to the other's leading questions he reaffirms
his moral position, emphasizing the function of the intellectual within the polity. How closely related the
Dialogue is to On Tyranny and to The Prince and
Letters is made more apparent by the exhortation to
"speak," if "doing" is precluded by the "vile govern-
ments" of the time, an injunction which echoes the
preface to On Tyranny.

As the brief work progresses, the emerging moral profile of the author becomes one with his programmatic
literary perspective. The theme of how difficult it is
to translate forte sentire ("strong feeling") from
one's inner being into literature is emphasized in a
lightly polemical vein aimed at contemporary fashions of
writing. "Great words" are not necessarily great deeds.
The only possible way to transmit to others the personal
experience of the "beautiful," the "warmth of the soul,"
is through "natural simplicity"—that simplicity, of
course, that was the essence of Alfieri's own stylistic
doctrine. A major motif is the idea that an individual's
soul can benefit and soar by deeply "feeling" something
even without "doing" it. This is when the writer comes
in, for he makes it possible for the reader to "feel"
great emotions.

A similar statement contained in The Prince inferred
that a writer, to give life to a great character, must
possess all of the high moral and intellectual qualities
of his protagonists; and, further, that "in general a man
who wrote well would, other things being equal, surpass a
man who acted well" (6). Such a creed is at the basis of
all of Alfieri's programs. The essential function of the
poet was thus expressed in The Prince, where the author
did in fact underscore his preference for the pen over
the sword. He firmly believed that "the pen in the hand

of a skillful writer is a more powerful and fearful weapon, and more lasting in its effects, than any sceptre or sword in the hand of a prince" (7). Going one step further, Alfieri stated that he could recognize the greatness of a man in the execution of a "sublime" deed, but that he saw a double greatness in the spirit who was able to describe it in a "sublime" fashion.

The poet's interlocutor therefore exhorts him to express all of his noble resentment (<u>bile</u>, "bile") through his writings. Such wrath could be the best lesson to offer to the people if used with discretion and subtlety. Dante's poetics come immediately to mind, the main difference being that the Florentine author did not resort to precautionary measures: his lesson was intended to sting! Care should be taken, however, not to apply the didactic method too directly and openly, for then it would become offensive and lose its effectiveness. The poet should "think" with the great authors of antiquity and write as if he were to be read by them only. Simplicity of style, combined with loftiness of thought, could be achieved in the writing of tragedies; these, he is instructed, should represent his major care, not the poems. What Italy needed was spiritual strength, not the "sweetness of sighs."

The paradigm reflected a practical, personal aspect of Alfieri's literary life. Precisely at that moment Alfieri was engrossed in the revision and publishing of his theatrical works, and also in reorganizing, correcting, and eventually printing his lyric poetry. A corollary to this reassessment of his activity is made up by the suggestion that he put an end to the composition of original works, and dedicate the rest of his life to the polishing (Alfieri uses the humanistic metaphor of the file) of what he had produced in the "furor" (<u>bollore</u>) of his youthful years. This advice was followed by the poet only partially.

The inner consistency of Alfieri's ideals finds a concise expression in his <u>Panegyric</u>, a brief work held together externally by a precise and tight subdivision into ten chapters. Internally, it is animated by the combination of its imaginative dimension with a typical coherence of vision. Its harmonious concurrence with the author's aspirations makes it exemplary of this period of intense self-scrutiny. Once more, extrinsic tensions and pressing political and moral issues are translated into a literary form.

Pliny the Younger becomes the voice of the poet's
conscience, the expression of his quest for liberty.
Rather than stating his argument in terms of the true
reality of the political scene of his time, Alfieri chose
to project his dream of freedom onto the stage of the
Roman Empire under Trajan. The link between the two historical moments, however, is established from the very
beginning. Pliny describes a sharp contrast between the
glory of the past and the miserable degeneration of the
present. Such a comparison makes it unavoidable for a
good citizen to become fearful of his own time and to
long for the past (8). The implied but obvious analogy
gives Alfieri, by choosing an ancient Roman spokesman,
the opportunity to express himself in a more elevated
tone, on the same stylistic level as his tragic production. Nonetheless, it soon becomes apparent that this is
a utopian vision of society. We have entered the speculative realm of the "what if?"

Critics are usually anxious to point out Alfieri's
predilection for Machiavelli. Earlier in this work, in
fact, we pointed out the poetics of simplicity of style
that seem to be common to both writers. However, in the
Panegyric Alfieri is at the opposite pole from
Machiavelli's Prince. In his Prince the Florentine
writer was giving advice on how to conquer, retain, or
expand one's dominions. Alfieri's Pliny, on the contrary, exhorts Trajan to relinquish his imperial status,
to become a citizen among citizens—to restore freedom to
Rome. The benefits that all would derive from the
restored liberty are then envisioned. The stylistic tone
has all the flavor of a prophetic utterance. The armies
are disbanded; the laws are restored to their ancient
validity; everyone is anxious to emulate the other's good
deeds; everyone is fired by the desire to acquire peren-
nial fame through the nobility of his actions. The
father can embrace his sons and daughters with the cer-
tainty that no one and nothing can harm them. In such a
world the rich would no longer fear for the safety of
their treasures; the poor would work to enrich themselves
with a new sense of civic dignity and worth. Furthermore, freedom would inspire orators in the Forum with
lofty subjects. No hero could be judged as greater than
Trajan, should he choose to follow Pliny's advice.

Could the pessimist Alfieri really believe that such a
society could exist? Perhaps not, but it is precisely

his yearning after the dream of such a world that made
him a poet, not a politician.

The Two Brutuses

Two new tragedies of liberty are born from this rekin-
dling of ideals. Alfieri had been prompted by his desire
to go one better than Voltaire, who had composed a tragedy on the subject of Brutus, to conceive the two works
simultaneously. In the process he also discovered that
the two subjects were particularly suited to his imagination. Unfortunately, after the great creations of Saul
and Myrrha, the Brutus works appear anticlimactic. Too
close to the author's theoretical writings, they are
hindered by their programmatic abstract nature. They do
not reach the intense level of conflicting tensions that
was attained in other tragedies of liberty such as Virginia, Timoleon, or the Conspiracy of the Pazzi.
Following his predilection for the symmetry of opposites,
Alfieri chose two episodes from the history of Rome that
had a common denominator—the love for liberty—and that
were symbolically differentiated by the fact that one
took place at the beginning of the Republic, the other at
its end, with the birth of the Roman Empire. As Alfieri
put it, "one at the birth of Rome, and the other at its
death" (9). In the first episode a father must sacrifice
his two sons to ensure the freedom of the state; converse-
ly, in the other one, the same situation compels the son
to slay his father.

The first Brutus is Lucius Junius Brutus, one of the
first two consuls of the Roman Republic, and the man
responsible for the expulsion of the Tarquins in 507 B.C.
The second is Marcus Junius Brutus, the slayer of Caesar
in 44 B.C. The first work was dedicated to George Washington, "the liberator of America," and the other to the
Italian people "of the future." Significant structural
elements common to both plays are: the absence of female
characters, a more active participation of the Roman
people, and the fact that the action culminates with the
triumph of libertarian ideals, but without the immolation
of the hero.

As it did in Merope, this last trait constitutes a
drastic departure from the usual disastrous conclusion of
Alfieri's tragedies. Such a climax is intended to convey

a sense of satisfactory retribution, but the drama loses most of its pathos. The atmosphere of inescapable doom that had magnificently characterized Alfieri's best works is absent in these two, rather frigid tragedies. Even the least touch of would-be optimism seems not to befit our poet's Muse. The two Brutuses, fettered by their exemplary, monochromatic purpose, become mere vehicles for the author's libertarian aspirations.

The First Brutus (which in the poet's opinion is the better play), at least, preserves an affective dimension that makes the characterization of the protagonist somewhat more acceptable as a poetic creation. Lucius Brutus loves his sons, Titus and Tiberius, yet he has to be inflexible. He must "pre- pare to render to assembled Rome / A cruel, fierce, unparallel'd example / Of desp'rate fortitude" [4.2]. Titus and Tiberius had been enticed, under false pretenses, to join the conspirators favorable to the restoration of the Tarquins' rule over Rome. Now they have to be punished along with the others. The father is dismayed, but his love for liberty —his strongest point, but the weakest element within the economy of the tragedy—must override any possible alternative. It is the ever-recurring situation of the conflicting dual role: "Unhappy Brutus! . . . / Thou art no more a father . . . but thou'rt yet / Consul, no less than citizen of Rome" [4.3]. The sacrificial blood has to be spilled, which is all the more precious for being the blood of his children: ". . . Fix ye on them your eyes: now Rome / Free and eternal rises from that blood" [5.2]. Once the sacrifice is consummated and the liberty of the new republic is ensured, the father can state: "I am the most unhappy man that ever lived." His dream of freedom has come true, but at what a price!

The Second Brutus lacks any motif of true affection as a basic ingredient of the action and, therefore, any possible inner tension. As in Sophonisba, Alfieri was relying entirely on the historical grandiosity of the figures involved, but this allowed him to attain only a rhetorical dimension, not a tragic one.

Alfieri's vein as a tragic author had come to an end. He himself wrote a brief, meaningful farewell to the tragic actor's footwear, the buskin, which becomes a metonymy for the profession of dramatic author:

> Reason enjoins me from my feet to doff
> (If I e'er wore it) the Italian buskin,

And I swear that I will never don it more.

(Anno <u>MDCCLXXXVII</u>)

Toward an Idealized Self-Portrait

The <u>Rime</u> (<u>Poems</u>) which Alfieri had been readying for publication saw the light in the Kehl edition of 1789. The bulk of this <u>canzoniere</u> was made up of 188 sonnets, two <u>canzoni</u>, one "Anacreontic" composition, one <u>capitolo</u> (literally, "chapter") in tercets, two series of stanzas in ottava rima, and forty-four epigrams. All of these poems were written between 1766 and 1780 (10). We know that Alfieri had written at least one love sonnet as far back as 1770, and in his <u>Vita</u> he mentions yet another sonnet, written on the memorable occasion of his freeing himself from the passion for the <u>odioso-amata</u> ("hated and loved") lady in 1775 (11). The author felt that these, and many other poems, were not worthy of publication, and they were not included in the Kehl edition. Later, Alfieri prepared a second collection of his poetry, covering the period 1789-1798. This was published posthumously in 1804, by Piatti, in Florence, with the false indication of London (12).

The first part of the <u>Rime</u> constitutes the best possible connecting link between the tragedies and the prose works, on the one hand, and the autobiography that will shortly follow. For that matter, the sonnets, insofar as they make up a kind of poetical diary, served as the initial basis for the more minute search for "time past" represented by the <u>Vita</u>. From a strictly aesthetic point of view, the <u>Rime</u>, with rare exceptions, are rather mediocre. Had Alfieri's fame rested solely on them, he would probably be remembered as simply one of the many minor versifiers of that era. As they are only a small part of his literary output, they are useful in that they illustrate his constant stylistic search. They fulfill an intimately felt need to channel his exuberant emotional and intellectual experiences into severely restricted metrical forms. Alfieri's sense of self-discipline is revealed once more in his choice of lyric meters. In the tragedies his natural ebullience was given a sense of order and measure by the overall organicity of structure of the classical theater he had adopted. Within that framework, however, his creative spirit could still enjoy the ductile freedom of the traditional

eleven-syllable line and of blank verse. The precise
architecture of the sonnet compensates for the more fluid
nature of the diaristic experience.

Alfieri's models were not only Plutarch, Dante, and
Machiavelli, but a great poet of the Italian lyrical tradition, Petrarch (1304-1374), cast his shadow over his
heart. Ariosto (1474-1533), Tasso (1544-1595)—even
Poliziano (1454-1494)—are all very present in Alfieri's
verses, but the true exemplum mentis in his Rime is
the author of the Canzoniere. Going beyond the superficial and formalistic imitation of Petrarch that was so
widespread in Italian poetry of the eighteenth century,
Alfieri shares the fundamental introspection that had
characterized the cantor of Laura. Romantically he felt
an emotional affinity for the melancholy portrayal of
nature as a projection of the poet's ever-shifting moods.
He accepted, furthermore, the concept that the only true
source of lyrical poetry is pianto, weeping or sorrow
caused by real passion. Alfieri looked beyond the rhetorical dimension of Petrarch's poetry to its essence,
which responded to the imperative necessity of self-
narration. The yearning for self-knowledge, which is at
the basis of Alfieri's Rime, culminates in the well-
known self-portrait [Sonnet 168]. It is as if the whole
long series of poems had been aiming at this from the
start. Finally, the poet confronts himself directly:
"Sublime specchio di veraci detti / Mostrami in corpo e
anima qual sono" (Thou mirror of veracious speech sublime
/ What I am like in soul and body, show). The image of
the mirror is the key word and sends us back to the
poet's search for self-identity. This identity will be
portrayed, on a much larger scale, in his Vita, in
which his literary search for authenticity finds one of
its greatest vehicles of expression.

Achilles and Thersites

The ideal date of Alfieri's autobiography—La Vita di
Vittorio Alfieri da Asti scritta da esso (The Life of
Vittorio Alfieri of Asti Written by Himself)—is the
year 1790. Even if the author later introduced large-
scale stylistic emendations and added—starting in 1798
and continuing until a short time before his death in
1803—a second, brief part, it is the year 1790 that
remains the most significant moment in our critical per-

spective. In the same year Alfieri began to sketch a
prospectus of his literary activity with the mock-serious
title of Rendimento di conti da darsi al Tribunal
d'Apollo sul buon o mal impiego degli anni virili, dal
1774 in poi (A rendering of accounts to be delivered
before the Court of Apollo on the good or evil use of his
adult years, from 1774 on). These literary annals thus
started from the crucial date of 1774 and were eventually
destined to continue until 1802. To all of this he added
a project for future works up to the year 1806; it was
facetiously entitled L'uom propone e Dio dispone (Man
proposes and God disposes) (13).

Alfieri had finished the revision and publication of
all of his completed works and was now ready to confront
himself directly. The sonnet containing his self-portrait
had posed a tremendously challenging question: "Uom, se'
tu grande, o vil? Muori, e il saprai" (Man, art thou
great or vile? Die, and, thou'lt learn!). Stepping down
from the rhetorical level of those epigrammatic conclud-
ing verses and abandoning their tone of finality, Alfieri
could now formulate his own self-assessment. The answer
that will emerge is condensed in his Introduction to the
Vita. Here, the two antithetical terms "great" (Achilles) or "vile" (Thersites) are transposed onto the more
general level of bene ("good") and male ("bad").
Alfieri had become certain that the amount of good in his
life is superior to that of his negative opposite. This
aesthetical, as well as moral, self-judgment is one primary key to the interpretation of his autobiography. The
familiar dichotomy of good and evil, the dialectical tension between positive and negative, are now disguised
within the alternating experiences of the author. But
which experiences? Alfieri could include in his Vita
only those events that he regarded as symptomatic of a
certain personal profile he wanted to trace of himself.
The literary fabric of the autobiography is not that of a
novel; it has all the texture of reinterpretation. Various episodes of his life are, at a later time, reassessed
and given a particular value according to an opinion that
the author had by then acquired of himself.

As for many other memoirs of the eighteenth century,
it is not a question of whether we accept or reject its
veracity. The events portrayed are real enough. The
sincerity of an idealized self-portrait is what the
reader must accept. The idealization itself was a true
reality in the mind of the author.

According to The Prince and Letters, the poet must
partake of all the characters he creates. Reversing the
concept, it becomes obvious that some traits of every
invented character converge into the new "character" of
the Vita. The presence of diverse personages can thus
be felt, at given moments, in the heartbeat of the
Vita's protagonist. In Alfieri's case, the axiom and
its reverse must be evaluated in the light of a passage
from Aristotle's Poetics. Elaborating on how to represent characters, Aristotle says: "Again, since tragedy
is an imitation of persons who are above the common
level, the example of good portrait painters should be
followed. They, while reproducing the distinctive form
of the original, make a likeness which is true to life
and yet more beautiful" (14). Clearly Alfieri followed
the same "example." He produced the "distinctive form of
the original," yet he tipped the balance in favor of the
"good" he mentions in his Introduction. He improved on
the "true-to-life" facts with suggestions of the "more
beautiful" already developed in his theater.

His Giornali (Journals, November, 1774) begin by
recognizing that, in the majority of cases, "se rendre
compte à soi-meme des actions de chaque jour" (to answer
oneself of one's own everyday actions) is a waste of
time, for one always repeats the same errors. Nonetheless, the author argues in the same paradoxical and facetious vein that it could be that, by analyzing himself,
he could learn to tolerate better his own personality
(15). The Journals were relatively short-lived—from
1774 to 1777. They lacked a supportive structure, and
their entries were sporadic. The writer began in French,
and then shifted to Italian. They were also wanting in
that basic functional axis of the Vita: its overall
perspective.

Apart from these organic reasons for failure, the personage the author was trying to define day by day was too
elusive. Alfieri had not yet created his masterpieces;
the autobiographical "I" was only potentially related to
the actions of the historical characters he was becoming
so fascinated with, and close to emotionally. Only after
writing tragedies, lyric poetry, and other works; only
after anchoring his passion to one person, could he
achieve a more penetrating grasp on his restless self.
He had lived a life with a purpose; a crescendo of practical experiences had already borne certain fruits: the
acquisition of knowledge and the conscious acceptance and
rejection of political convictions.

Again, in the very first sentence of the Introduction
to his Vita Alfieri declares that writing about oneself
is prompted by "self-love." This particular kind of self-
love is a precious gift that allows a man aware of his
own ability and limits to achieve greatness. Furthermore, having acquired some fame, the author fears that
someone less well informed might be tempted to write
about him. Better, then, to do it himself. Under this
whimsical pretense of practical reasons lies the urgent
necessity for autobiographical expression that was, for
Alfieri, the essential calling in writing.

The particular way he looked at writing about himself
—namely, his intention to probe more deeply into the perception of his own person, while at the same time projecting a self-portrait to the world, the lively interaction,
then, of acquiring and transmitting self-knowledge—is
alluded to in a revealing sentence in the last paragraph
of the Journals. There, on Tuesday, June 3, 1777, he
affirmed that: "First of all, I want to appear handsome;
then rich; then a man of wit; then an author and a man of
genius. I am placing my batteries for that purpose: I
shall say later with what results" (16). He was speaking
at the time about a particular situation, but his preoccupation with presenting himself "in a favorable light," as
he put it, was a constant throughout his life. The "I
shall say later" proposition alludes schematically to an
eventual portrait of the author that faithfully reflects
that program. The fragmentary, but richly detailed picture of Alfieri that emerges from the numerous letters to
relatives and friends is not discordant with the Vita.
But the poet's correspondence, though true to the same
basic aspects of his personality, lacks the emphatic
tone, the interpretive quality, and the overall architecture of a complete, finished work, which the autobiography is.

A Reinterpretation of the Past

The Vita was intended to be divided into five parts,
each structurally corresponding to one of the five ages
of man: childhood, adolescence, youth, virility, and old
age. The analogy of this subdivision with the five acts
of traditional tragedy was dictated by that same sense of
self-discipline that ruled the "unruly" spirit of the
author. The fifth age having never been written (or
reached), the Vita encompasses four epoche ("epochs").

The first spans the years from 1749 to 1758, from birth
to age nine, "nine years of vegetation"; the second epoch
(1758-1766) covers "eight years of ineducation" from nine
to seventeen; the third epoch (1766-1775) embraces "approximately ten years of travels and dissipation" from
seventeen to twenty-six; finally, from twenty-six to
forty-one (1755-1790), the period of virility, embraces
"thirty and more years of compositions, translations, and
diverse studies."

In retracing the evolution of Alfieri's poetics and
the establishment of his method of composition (the
genesis, in short, of his tragedies), we had the opportunity—indeed we were compelled—to draw profusely upon
the fourth part of the Vita. We must now concentrate
on the first three epochs because, in them, the author
sought to unearth the roots of his personality and the
foundation of the poet-to-be. In this respect, the conclusion of the five rather brief chapters that make up
the first part of the book is of extreme interest.

Alfieri wrote that the description of his first nine
years of life might, perhaps, be considered useless by
all those who, "regarding themselves as men, seem to
forget that man is a continuation of the child" (17).
This statement combines a multiplicity of meanings.
First, it is a clear indication of Alfieri's interest in
psychological analysis, which, in turn, confirms his disposition for introspection and explains his desire to
decipher his own personality. Further, since the image
of the child that emerges from the account is undoubtedly
sketched with a view to explaining the man who was to
become his continuation, the privilege of choice that the
author has granted himself, with regard to the events he
relates, immediately reveals its predetermined, selective
principle.

A symptomatic example of the author's attitude is to
be found at the very beginning of the narrative. He
declares himself to be thankful for being born into an
aristocratic family because this gave him the opportunity
to criticize, and even chastise, the nobility of his
times without incurring the risk of appearing merely
envious and vile. As is his wont, the author is evalu-
ating the past in the light of his present convictions.
To round out the perspective on his fate-willed birth, he
then brings wealth into the picture. Riches made him, he
says, "pure and free." They made it possible for him to
serve no one, nothing but "Truth." This is the method of

reasoning which allowed him to eliminate the slightest
sense of guilt from his retrospective interpretation.

After writing only a few paragraphs, he has already
revealed a great deal about himself. Better yet, we have
ascertained his point of view. No less significant in
Alfieri's highly selective procedure is the withholding
of personal data. One of the areas that is left in the
vague penumbra of non-interpretation is the death of his
father. Alfieri relates how his father died, without
going any further into his own reaction. He describes
how, as a baby, he had been entrusted to the care of a
wet nurse, who lived approximately two miles from the
Alfieri residence, and how his father would walk that distance almost every day in order to see him. We are told
that, by the time Vittorio was about one year old, his
father—who was over sixty—fell ill as a consequence of
such exertion and passed away. Not too long thereafter,
the mother—who had been left with child by her husband—
remarried.

Although Alfieri refrains from elaborating and speculating on the loss of his father, this episode has great
significance. There is, in his narration, an implicit
sense of guilt which he will never overcome or even
acknowledge. If we add to this the subsequent depriva-
tion of both paternal love and authority, we can better
understand the inner congruence of many details in the
self-portrait which the author is at some pains to inter-
pret, in his own way, for the reader. These are the set
of germinal occurrences that predetermine the fundamental
peculiarities of his character; his melancholy inclination, his insufferance of authority, his constant need of
love and search for affection. We do not intend to
follow the path of a full psychological analysis of the
Vita, but to hint, nonetheless, at the possibility of
opening different perspectives into the reading of this
work.

After a brief excursion into the realm of "the affinity of thoughts with sensations," which reflects the
sensism of Lockian extraction which had been made popular
in Italy by the Jesuit, Etienne de Condillac (1715-1780),
Alfieri places in the foreground of his childhood experiences his first dolore del cuore, heartache or affective sorrow. This was caused by the separation from his
sister Giulia, who had been sent to a convent. Alfieri
interprets the event as the initial discovery of his
"sensitive faculties." Speculating later on such an

experience, he came to the conclusion that all kinds of
love are regulated by the same emotional mechanism. It
is yet another example of interpolating past and present,
where the latter is seen as a corollary of the former.

As time is highly condensed in the narrative of this
epoch, all of the salient characteristics of his personality can be quickly gathered in their forming. The
distance between the narrating "I" and his presumably
objective childhood projection is shortened more and
more. We learn, in rapid succession, of his inclination
to study, of his melancholy disposition, of his passionate character, of his self-destructive instinct, exemplified by an attempted suicide with classical connotations.
We learn further of his extreme pride in his personal
appearance, of his stubbornness in not bending to anyone
else's will, and, lastly, of his incipient longing for
gallantry and glory.

The intervening eight years of adolescence are defined
as a period of "ineducation" and described as an epoch of
"infirmity, idleness, and ignorance" (18). They embrace
his experience in the Royal Academy of Turin, which during that portion of his life was his de facto home, and
they underscore the absence of a well-structured program
of literary readings. But this epoch, "ineducation" notwithstanding, gave Alfieri its epiphanic moments. The
author places them toward the end of this second segment
of the Vita. One of these moments came with the sense
of "liberation" he experienced when, on the occasion of
his sister's marriage to Count Giacinto di Cumiana,
Alfieri was granted a month's leave and freedom, which he
spent in Cumiana, a few miles from Turin. He acquired
there his first horse, and with it the taste for riding
which was to become one of the great passions of his
life. Another momentous event was the infatuation for a
married woman. In relating the exterior signs of this
affective experience Alfieri employs the well-known
phenomenology of love as described by Dante in the Vita
Nova and by Petrarch—though inexplicably he does not
make a direct reference to either one of the two famous
poets. What is relevant in this episode is the fact that
in reliving his first love experience, the author of the
Rime gives it new meaning through an overlay of literary associations, adjusting it to an entirely different
temper from the one it had when he actually lived it.

In rapid summary the author points out other references to his future personality: a natural inclination

toward justice and equality, an inborn "generosity of
soul." He read into these propensities the signs of a
"free being" and of his worthiness of being emancipated
(19). All the major ingredients of his character are
therefore present by the end of the period of the "adolescence," which culminates in his leaving the Academy.
In the third part of the narrative ("youth") they blend
in that spiritual and intellectual fermentation that
leads to maturity.

The third epoch, that designated giovinezza
("youth"), lasted for a rather protracted period of time,
from the age of seventeen until twenty-seven. It began,
auspiciously enough, with a year-long voyage throughout
the mosaic of states that studded the Italian peninsula.
The author's impressions of places, people, art, and politics are disorderly and kaleidoscopic. Now and then, however, a sharper emotional sensation impresses itself on
his heart; a more precise political or intellectual
design leaves a mark on his mind. In meeting Ferdinand
IV he recognizes in the countenance of the young king of
Naples the same physiognomy as that of other monarchs he
had previously met. From the observation he derives—in
a loosely Machiavellian fashion—a general rule: all
princes look the same and all courts are merely "antecham-
bers." He discovers within himself a first sign of
avarice. The impression is almost overstressed, and it
is hardly pursued at all later in the Vita. It forms
another area of silence, concealing habits of conduct
from which Alfieri was not exempt (20).

He continues to assimilate an enormous variety of
sensations that will only be deciphered later. Meanwhile, he is so anxious to visit the rest of Europe that
the Italian experience is regarded almost as a waste of
time. Eventually, he goes to France and there he is
charmed by theatrical performances, with his preference
going to comedy, not to tragedy. In Paris he is negatively impressed by the French women and their taste for
excessive makeup. He is even more negatively impressed
by Louis XV's supercilious bearing.

As the kaleidoscope keeps turning, new colors and new
effects offer themselves to his eyes. England, then
Holland—where he has his first important sentimental
adventure. His first friendship is also established in
the person of Don José D'Acunha, the Portuguese ambassador to Holland. Alfieri gave great importance to this
relationship, for it was through D'Acunha that he came to

know Machiavelli's works. Some of the fundamental ener-
gies of his personality, such as love, friendship, and
his literary tastes, evolve by integrating with each
other.

It is now that Alfieri posits a creative model in
which only love is credited with promoting a desire for
studying and the stirring of productive ideas in his
mind. This is observed in the sixth chapter of the third
epoch, although a similar remark occurs in the second
chapter of the same section. Following his method of
superimposition of past and present, Alfieri had become
aware—and this is the conceptual core of this part of
his Vita—that, at the time, he was still totally
ignorant of himself. He also felt incapable of any positive initiative. He was constantly under the spell of
his "melancholy disposition." Only many years later, he
writes, "I realized that at the same time, my heart must
be occupied by a worthy love, and my mind busy with a
noble task; and any time that one of the two was missing,
I was also incapable of the other, and I felt satiated,
bored, and upset more than I can say" (21). Only at the
summation of his autobiography could he say that. Had he
confided his melancholy moods to a diary, a letter, or
even a sonnet, the same events, the same experiences
could never have acquired the meaning they now have.

The facts are there, so real, that we draw from them
as from an historical source; yet they are all suffused
with that particular halo of idealization mentioned earlier. This is the story of a soul, and not simply that of
a man. The years follow one another in rhythmic succession, and the year is, in fact, the unit of time that
measures the ideal, as well as the real, dimension of
Alfieri's Vita. The inner dynamics of this dimension,
its more intimate motor and also its unifying force, is
the sense of urgency that moved Alfieri to know and
reveal himself. It is the same will to self-analysis
that we encountered in the characters of the tragedies.

As he nears the end of the third epoch, Alfieri has
traveled from one end of Europe to another, he has fallen
in and out of love, has established friendships, and has
read widely. The climactic moment of his youth will soon
be reached. It will be a manifold conclusion. By the
year 1773, in Turin, completely absorbed by women and
horses, but also by his first attempts at writing poetry,
he is still without any definite plan for the future.
The moment of truth is near. A fierce illness takes him

to the threshold of death. His recovery is a new birth,
both symbolically and in the sphere of reality, for he
will ask for, and obtain, dismissal from his military
post. He thereby achieves complete freedom from all
political or civil obligations. This form of freedom was
soon to be followed by another: his liberation from his
"unworthy" love. His erratic will, his undisciplined
energy had finally found a direction and a purpose in the
writing of his first tragic composition, Cleopatra. A
fuller realization of the self was at hand.

In illustrating Alfieri's "conversion" and the birth
of his theater, we followed quite closely the account
given in the fourth epoch of the Vita. Now our critical perspective has come to a point of convergence with
the author's own narrative. Both our previous account of
his works (chapters 1-4) and the first part of his Vita
culminate with the year 1790—the date of composition of
the first draft of the autobiography in Paris. The relatively brief Second Part, which Alfieri later added to
his work, takes the reader up to 1803, a few months
before his death, but the vital élan that had characterized the preceding pages is no longer present. The
chronicle of events only comes to life with the description of the author's escape from the enraged mob of
French revolutionaries. Its historical implications make
it indispensable to the student of the "late" Alfieri,
but the ideal self-portrait had been accomplished long
since.

Chapter Six
Disillusion

Alfieri's last thirteen years of life contrast with the preceding epochs of his life both in social behavior and creative activity. After escaping from Paris during the revolution of 1792, he took up residence in Florence with the Countess of Albany. They were never to leave their adopted city, except momentarily during the French occupation of 1799 and 1800 (1).

It is a different Alfieri we are now confronting. The writing of the autobiography and other miscellaneous literary efforts, together with the edition of the tragedies, and, above all, the experience of the French Revolution, left him mentally and physically exhausted. His disillusionment with humanity is deeper than ever. When the time comes for his indomitable creative urge to speak again, his new perspective is by turns satirical and comic. As early as 1780, in writing to his friend Mario Bianchi in Siena, Alfieri had declared his intention of shifting his interest to comedy. His accent reflected a growing skepticism concerning the "things of the world." At the time, Paris and the Parisians bored him, and he resolved that the only way to vent his discontent was through laughter, through comedy. He was thirty-eight then, and he was resolved that upon reaching forty he would definitely "shed the buskin, and with it the tears and the tragic mask; and I want to consecrate six more years, not more, to laughing at all worldly things, since perhaps they do not deserve anything else" (2). Not by chance then, starting in 1790, Alfieri devoted his energy to translating Terence, the Latin author of comedies. After the writing of the autobiography, translations from Latin (and later from Greek) had become his principal activity. His objective was twofold: to master the Latin of the great classical authors—the first in importance being Virgil—but also, by a study of the comic authors, to master a new expressive mode. Alfieri's intention was: "To create for myself a comic verse in order to write (as I had been planning for a long time) comedies of my own; and also to display, in this genre, a personal and original style, as I believed I had done in the tragedies" (3).

His plans were not carried out in chronological sequence, and many years went by before he could give life to his comic theater. Eventually, turning away from a Plutarchian idealization of man, Alfieri's later work peaks with a satiric and bitterly comic vision of the human lot in three overlapping phases: the Misogallo (The French-hater), the Satire (Satires), and the Commedie (Comedies). These works give the measure of Alfieri's disillusionment, but also of his perseverance. The composition of the Misogallo and of the Satire coincided so closely with each other that it was only for convenience that the author separated one from the other.

Misogallo

The external events that precipitated Alfieri's disillusionment must be identified with the excesses of the French Revolution, which he witnessed directly. At first, enthusiastic about the popular revolt, Alfieri had written an ode, Parigi sbastigliata (Un-bastilled Paris), to commemorate the capture of the infamous Bastille. What followed, however, put an unbearable stress on his libertarian ideals: the enraged populace of Paris did not resemble at all the rarefied image of the classical heroes that had populated his fantasy and his theater.

Even though he could understand and, to a certain extent, condone the bloodshed necessary for the establishment of a new social and political order, he could never accept the mundane and pragmatic ideology of the "cheap lawyers" leading the revolution (4). Alfieri remained fundamentally an aristocrat. The only plebeians he could envision as being capable of great and "noble" deeds belonged to the historical perspective of ancient Rome or Greece. The crude experience of a modern uprising could only shock him back to reality. The acrimony that exudes from the pages of the Misogallo must be viewed as an instinctive reaction to the sudden realization that ideals are ideals and can never be transposed to the level of pragmatic experience in all their purity.

Still, Alfieri was unable to accept fully "the effective reality of things," and his disenchantment takes the form of hatred toward the French. Whatever was base or vile in the revolution is for him, at this point, not the

result of behavior patterns typical of all men, but the
unique expression of a national trait. Hatred enabled
Alfieri, at least partially, to cope with the shattering
of his heroic, libertarian aspirations. A torrent of
embittered sonnets and epigrams issued then from the
poet's pen, as if in an attempt to "exorcise" reality.
Such was the conceptual genesis of the Misogallo, which
became an organic whole only with time. It crystallized
in 1798 when it acquired the finished form of a collection of verse held together by five prose essays, which
constitute de facto its ideological marrow.

The first prose piece is a dedication to past, present, and future Italy; the second gives the "reason" of
the work; the third is a "translation" of the last words
of Louis XVI to the National Convention; the fourth takes
the classical form of a dialogue between a free man and a
freed slave (liberto); the last is another dialogue
between the ghosts of Louis XVI and Robespierre (5).

In the first prose piece Alfieri justifies the hate that
should be nurtured in Italy against her "natural" enemy,
and from this nationalistic point of view he underscores
the creation of the neologism misogallo. But it is the
second piece that emerges as the most articulate and
exhaustive of the five in expressing the author's ideological shift. He warns the reader that he is not writing
history, but his "impressions" of it. For years, he had
depicted men as they could and should be, and now it
would actually be "sickening" for him to represent them
as they really are (6). Nonetheless, his "impressions"
could still serve the purpose of enhancing the memory of
the good and discrediting the bad. The early concept of
the usefulness of literature is thus charged with a new
vitality. The author proceeds on a very personal note,
summarizing his own intellectual and emotional experiences as a worshipper of freedom. In doing so, he
achieves the same tone he had attained when describing
his vision of a utopian society in his Panegyric of
Pliny. The depiction of a free and socially harmonious
humanity is then contrasted with a desolating appraisal
of the French people. We now learn, somewhat tautologi-
cally, that only the members of his imaginary society
could be "free and pure"—just and magnanimous men, who
could avoid falling into the pitfalls of envy, licen-
tiousness, and base vindictiveness. Although the author
is prepared to concede that it may be necessary to ac-

complish some "bad" in order to achieve the "good," the French had been incapable of even that.

It is legitimate now to ask, who are the French he is speaking about? The core of Alfieri's polemical tirades is, in fact, aimed against the emerging bourgeoisie, the "third estate." The author's ideological involution springs from his realization that the principle of equality, whatever he may have meant by it, cannot be easily realized, not can the ideals of liberty or moral virtue. The Plutarchian idealism that had nurtured Alfieri the man, as well as the poet, was not applicable to historical reality. The disdain he felt toward the French mob was the antagonism of the aristocrat toward a lower social class—a class which was not moved by uncontaminated ideals, but which was guided by a vile instinct for revenge.

Alfieri could not accept the restructuring of a society that allowed the worst kind of servitude—"the dependence, that is, of the owner, of the good, on the dispossessed and the criminal" (7). Had he witnessed a similar historical occurrence in Italy, his reaction would have undoubtedly been the same. The venomous verse and prose of the Misogallo does not rise to the aesthetic level of the author's preceding production. Its relevance is entirely documentary in its manifestation of the "late" Alfieri's disillusionment and the revision of the enthusiastic values of his youth.

The Satirical Approach

In the same period (1792–1798) Alfieri composed sixteen Satires. Even though the stylistic concern appears somewhat fastidious in its metric structure (the Dantesque terza rima typical of such compositions), the ideological genesis and its emotional projection remain the same as in the Misogallo. The major polemical target is still the French and the pernicious example they have set for the other European nations. Even though the Satires invest most social types and species —from kings to the plebs, or plebeians, to the sesqui-plebes, or plebeians and a half, Alfieri's term of scorn for the middle classes—and cover programatically a far wider polemical ground than the Misogallo, a constant, biting sarcasm is apparent from the very first. The

author's apostrophe to the "malign reader" is a penetrating injunction to read, at least, before condemning (8).
The pugnacious tone that constantly runs through this
verse is one of its outstanding features. The typically
Alfierian posture, disdainful and antagonistic, is apparent in the recurring use of the familiar personal pronoun
tu, which in Italian has the connotation that the person addressed is either a friend or a relative—or a
social inferior.

Alfieri's new ideological conservatism pervades I Re
(The kings), I Grandi (The great ones), La Plebe (The
plebs), and La Sesquiplebe (The sesqui-plebs). In I
Re the author—his critical eye still turned toward
France—affirms that: true, in order to "make" a good
king, one must first "unmake" the reigning monarch, but
he is quick to add that the move is essentially foolish
(stolt'opra) if the necessity then arises to "re-print"
another one. His final admonishment is "Solo osi i Re
disfare un Popol fatto" (Let only a fully made people
dare to unmake kings) (9).

That Alfieri's vision of the political polarization
between king and people should be more benevolent toward
the monarch should not come as a shocking revelation to
the attentive reader of his tragedies, in which the
elimination of the tyrant-king-father was never accomplished in order to bring about an essentially democratic
substitution of power, but always to replace one (evil)
individual with another (good) one. The author's deep-
rooted and constant concern was ultimately the cult of
individuality—an obsessive and narcissistic affirmation
of personality. Aristocracy remained the necessary
prerequisite. While chastising the nobility of his time,
Alfieri focused mainly on marginal issues, such as vanity
and lack of true political participation. As a whole, as
is apparent in I Grandi, the satirist recognizes the
basic privileges and rights of aristocracy. Following a
line of reasoning that seems to be inspired by Castigli-
one's Book of the Courtier, Alfieri posits the double
merit that can be attained by a nobleman when he adds the
glory of his own actions to that of his family tree (10).
Unfortunately, this can only be attained by the truly
grandi ("great"), and a survey of contemporary aris-
tocracies comes up with merely "pigmies." Hence, his
satirical depiction of aristocracy.

When dealing with the "plebs," Alfieri's satire
becomes more and more vitriolic. Opening with a verse
from Dante's Inferno, "La gente nuova, e i sùbiti

guadagni" (New men and sudden riches), the polemical
arrows are now aimed against the new rich: the
social climbers. The satirical composition acquires the
design of a veritable drama. It follows an imaginary
archetype from the basest of births, through a cunning
ascent to riches and power, to his death on the gallows
(11). The poet's indignation is triggered by the conviction that no parvenu can occupy the position of leader-
ship which belongs only to the aristocracy. The newly
rich bourgeois has no other privilege than to obey and to
serve.

While he remains highly critical of the political
ideology that upholds the principle of sovereignty of the
people, and is leery of the system of democratic representation, it is the lawyers, merchants, and writers of the
ceto medio ("middle class"), who are judged, from
Alfieri's moral point of view, to be the più brutti
("the ugliest") (12). In striking out at them, he is, in
fact, aiming at the very leaders of the social revolution
he had witnessed in France. He represents them as being
the lowest stratum of society because they are parasites
who gain their sustenance at the expense of others.
After witnessing this process of involution, we can now
return to one of the opening statements of the Vita and
see in a different light what Alfieri meant by pronoun-
cing himself to be "pure" and "free" for having been born
into wealth. In the context of the Satires, the same
concept acquires a negative value. Only the rich aristocrat, by spending his own patrimony without the necessity
of work, does not cause any harm to anyone. By occupying
such a privileged position, according to Alfieri, he is
unquestionably less vile, "men sozzo," than those who are
his social inferiors (13).

Alfieri's reactionary stance is intensified in L'Anti-
religioneria (The anti-religion fashion) and in La
Filantropineria (The philanthropic fashion). In the
first we can feel the author's sense of polemical satisfaction in squaring off against the eighteenth-century
gallic spirit personified by Voltaire. In a romantic
defense of "illusion" against the crudity of "rationality" Alfieri takes the opposite position from his stance
when writing On Tyranny, where he regarded religion as
one of the pillars of tyrannical power. Here he vindi-
cates the necessity of the comforting function of religion within the social fabric. The poet's concern is not
theology, but the practical functionality of faith. It
provides a structure that, being integrated with the

established order, tends to prevent, to some extent, possibly corrupting or subversive processes (14). Similar-
ly, in La Filantropineria Alfieri—still using France
as a term of comparison—sarcastically mocks what he considers a false example of a man's concern for his fellow-
man. In this perspective we are given to understand the
fallacy of eliminating the death penalty, an act that
implied deeper concern for the criminal than pity for his
hapless victim (15). A burning issue at the time, it had
been highly publicized and debated throughout Europe,
especially following the publication of Cesare Beccaria's
Dei delitti e delle pene (On Crime and Punishment) in
1764.

The reform of the political system constituted one of
the dividing lines between new and old social structures;
a testing ground which divided the reformers from the
conservatives (16). Symptomatically, Alfieri stood with
the latter group. This is also seen in the satire Le
Leggi (Laws), where he deplores the custom of axilum
("sanctuary"), the shelter offered by the Church to anyone who sought it, no matter how heinous his crimes had
been. In this composition the tragic poet's touch flares
up briefly when he describes the scene of a murderer
wiping the blood, still dripping from his dagger, as he
stands in front of a church altar (17).

With Il Commercio (Commerce) Alfieri denounces the
greed that pushes man toward vile commercial activity and
sordid economic ventures. His tirade against the spice
trade is reminiscent of Parini's bitter verses that evoke
the slaughter of the Aztecs and the Incas. This slaughter contributed to the enrichment of the aristocracy's
tables with coffee and cocoa (18). The subversion of old
established values again determines Alfieri's resistance
to the sweeping wave of modern mercantilism. In short,
he was condemning the inevitable outcome of all those
social, political, and economic changes that the ideology
of the Enlightenment had precipitated, the same ideology
to which he had enthusiastically subscribed in his youth.
The dramatic chasm that separated the ideal from reality
was too deep for him to cross. Ironically, he could not
detect the tragic potential, the "nobility," even in
human terms, inherent in the strife for the survival of
the fittest. The perspective that was to open up major
areas of existential preoccupation and major forms of
artistic expression in the culture of the following
century eluded him.

The author was aware of his ideological turnabout.
Writing to his friend Caluso, he recognized that what he
had once said had been dictated by a sincere faith in the
efficacy of truth, or what he then believed to be truth,
and that his purpose had always been to be "useful."
Now, in the present circumstances, he is ready to admit
that the damage stemming from such an attitude could out-
weigh its advantages. Thus, while willing to grant his
former principles a spontaneous and honest birth, he
again negates their utility. This is tantamount to recognizing their inadequacy in the face of reality (19).

The Comic Mask

While continuing to work on his translations and his
study of Latin and Greek, Alfieri kept alive his penchant
for autobiography. In verse, he continued to enrich his
diary of Petrarchan sonnets, which eventually became the
second part of the Rime (1799). Furthermore, in 1798
he had broken the seal that had protected the privacy of
the Vita manuscript; simultaneously he had begun a
stylistic revision of it and the writing of its final
segment (20). From the prose as well as from the verse
(and especially from the fascinating annotations that
accompany the verse, which give indications as to where,
when, and how they were written) a telling portrait of
the "late" Alfieri comes to life: a brooding, solitary
man, given to lonely walks and horseback rides along the
ancient walls of Florence, on the banks of the Arno and
its surrounding hills. "Satiated and disillusioned with
worldly matters; frugal and always dressed in black," he
undoubtedly cut a striking figure on the Florentine
social scene of the turn of the century (21). The young
Ugo Foscolo was so impressed with the Count that he cited
him as the prototype of the Romantic hero in his epistolary novel, Le ultime lettere di Jacopo Ortis (Last
Letters of Jacopo Ortis), and in the poem Dei Sepolcri
(On Sepulchres). Alfieri's misanthropy reached its
peak when he affixed on the door of his residence the following cantankerous and defiant notice: "Inasmuch as
Vittorio Alfieri is not a public person and imagines he
is entitled to be his own master at least in his own
house, he informs anyone who might be looking for him
that he never receives either people, messages, packages,
or letters from people he does not know, or to whom he is

not beholden." The warning was unceremoniously headed: "Vittorio Alfieri to the importunate visitor" (22).

The Vita states that in September, 1800, Alfieri felt impelled by a "natural and very strong impulse" to conceive six comedies—all at one birth. A further detail mentioned is trifling only in appearance. Alfieri declares he had in mind to write a total of twelve comedies, which is the same number of tragedies he had at first planned to compose (23). Together with the fateful date of 1800, marking the transition from one century to another, the resolution is more than revealing as to Alfieri's intentions. By returning to the theater under a different mask, he could finally make true the promise he had made to himself in 1786 and written to his friend Bianchi. An early penchant for the "comic" had been revealed long before, as far back indeed as his first attempt at tragedy, Cleopatra, first drafted in 1744. That first tragedy had in fact been accompanied by a farce, I Poeti (The poets), where the author, in what amounts to a self-parody, had experimented with what he claimed was his "innate" sense of humor. That side of his personality, the Thersites that complemented his Achilles, was kept alive through the years by a recurring theoretical interest in the comic (24).

The first six works of the planned dozen were intended to provide examples of three distinct types of comedy. The initial group of four (he considered them as one play divided into four parts) dealt with comic situations universally recurring in any epoch, place, and society; the fifth dealt with "fantastic and poetical" situations, in a wide, temporal, sociopolitical perspective; the sixth comedy was to focus on the andamento moderno to close in on "modern trends." Alfieri stated polemically that his century, somewhat wanting in inventiveness, with its bourgeois heroes and its stress on the poignant aspects of its comic situations, had attempted in vain to "fish tragedy out of comedy." He, on the contrary, felt it to be more "useful, amusing, and verisimilar" to follow an opposite procedure, "fishing comedy out of tragedy," for "we can often see great and powerful personages that make us laugh; . . . but we can never feel any admiration for bankers, lawyers, and such" (25).

Following the same method of three-stage composition he had implemented in the writing of the tragedies, Alfieri worked at his comedies until the day of his death. The action of the comic works is not centered on

one or a few main characters (as it had been in the tragedies); instead, it is distributed among several of them.
Linguistically and thematically, as was to be expected,
the comedies are closer to the Misogallo, the Satires, and Epigrams than to the tragedies. The style
alternates among the discursive, reflexive, and polemical
modes, a fluctuation often amplified by being set in a
colloquial verbal mold. They brim with bizarre neolo-
gisms; besides the example of Terence, they reveal the
influence of Aristophanes, whose works Alfieri had recent-
ly been translating, and even Machiavelli—whose prose
comedy Mandragola he had partially put into verse (26).
But his muse would not allow him to dwell on the common,
simply making indulgent fun of the mediocre aspects of
life. Thus, whereas in the tragedies his imagination had
soared with the highest ideals of a humanity heroically
conceived, in his comedies it bitterly sneers at the
misery of reality.

An even deeper pessimism is barely concealed under the
comic mask. It is not so much that the poet had rejected
his ideals as that reality had undone them: this is what
made him bitter, vindictive, and, in the end, so sad.

Of Political Failure

The tetralogy mentioned above, which consists of
L'Uno (The one), I Pochi (The few), I Troppi (The
too many), and L'Antidoto (The antidote), constitutes
"a comedy in twenty acts," dealing with the three main
forms of government: i.e., monarchy, oligarchy, and
democracy. Each constitutional solution is considered
defective, hence the solution proposed by the "antidote,"
namely, a combination of all three. What again stands
out is Alfieri's concern for sociopolitical, and particularly institutional, issues. It is possible that he
derived his overall inspiration from Machiavelli's
Discorsi sulla prima Deca di Tito Livio (Discourses on
the First Ten Books of Titus Livius), in which the Florentine writer touches specifically on this question (27).
As for the characters and situations and historical
settings—ancient Persia, Greece, and Rome—critics have
pointed out that Alfieri was indebted to Herodotus for
L'Uno and to Plutarch for I Pochi and I Troppi
(28). However, we must add that by that time Alfieri's
assimilation of classical authors—ancient and modern—

was so great that it is impossible to separate in his
works Aristophanes from Terence, and Herodotus from
Machiavelli. The invention of the plots was entirely
his.

The action of the comedies does not possess the organic unity that characterizes the dramatic unfolding of the
tragedies. Lacking the intensity that only strong passion concentrated in one or two characters could gener-
ate, it tends to be fragmented and dispersive. This may
have been a device—we suggest—to exemplify the lack of
political coherence that a nation displays when it is
pressed to choose a given political structure. L'Uno
presents ten characters which include a soothsayer, a
high priest, a stable boy, and even a horse. After the
slaying of the usurper, the false Smerdi, Persia needs a
new king. There are seven pretenders, but only four
appear on the scene: Orcane, Darius (the future king),
Megabize, and Gobria. After a succession of minor episodes of intrigue, the high priest proposes that the
contenders meet on the field of battle at dawn. The one
whose horse neighs first will be recognized as the new
king.

In Alfieri's ironical bias the choice of this expedient is supposed to demonstrate the supernatural origin of
monarchy, whereas in reality it mocks it. This motif is
further tinged with sarcasm by the vulgar, yet shrewd
scheme of Ippofilo, Dario's stable boy, to insure the
victory of his master (a subterfuge involving the excre-
tions of a mare in heat [5.4]).

As a political play, L'Uno contains very little
philosophizing and even less speculative thought, but
this is true of the other comedies as well; indeed it is
true of almost all comedy. In the end, if anything,
L'Uno highlights the "fatal necessity," or inevitabili-
ty, of monarchy. The character who comes through as the
most noble and who bears a melancholy resemblance to
Alfieri's tragic heroes, is not the winner, Dario, but
rather Gobria, who chooses not to participate in the
struggle and opts for a self-imposed exile.

In I Pochi Alfieri aimed at chastising the oligar-
chic form of government, but again he falls short of
transforming his political object into a work of art. At
first, he thought of setting the action against the background of the political scene of Venice, but then he
chose Rome (29). The target of the author's satire is
embodied in the famous historical figures of Tiberius

Graccus and his brother Caius. They are trying to elect
the plebeian Gloriaccino consul, in order to make him
their puppet. A secondary plot is provided by the maneu-
vering of Caius Graccus, who wants to win Mitulla away
from the Tribune Furiaccino and marry her himself. More
than in the preceding play, the Plutarchian characters
are here morally devalued and appear merely as scheming
demagogues. The implied comparison with the pettifogging
lawyers of the Misogallo is very clear. The least
tarnished figure is again an aristocrat, Fabius, who
stands out for his moderation and good sense. Even this
straightforward satire does not end up as a condemnation
of the aristocracy, but rather as the contrary (30).

I Troppi contains some of the best moments in
Alfieri's comic production. The arrangement of the
action has a wider orchestration; the language is freer,
more pungent, and the various incidents are presented
dynamically. Alfieri himself was rather satisfied with
his effort and was prompted to affirm: "I am certain
that this is where the comedy is. Though foolish modern
authors may have decided to bring tragedy into the tav-
ern, with their middle-class dramas, I am convinced that
better results can be achieved by bringing comedy into
the palace, where it can in fact live comfortably" (31).
In accordance with his poetics of "distance" Alfieri
abandoned the idea of using the French Revolution as a
background and elected instead to set I Troppi at the
court of Alexander the Great. The action is simple:
eight ambassadors from Athens go to Babylon to ingratiate
their country with the Persian emperor. They are led by
the famous orators Demosthenes and Aeschines. The distor-
tion of the classical ideal of composure and eloquence is
immediately revealed, as in the other plays, by the grotesque names Alfieri has given to many of the characters,
such as Onisco, Miosco, Muisco, Coirisco, and Aspalisco,
where the repetition of the meaningless, but foolishly
exotic-sounding -isco binds them together in a bitter
parody of pomp and distinction. The deformation of reality by means of bizarre phonemes is, in fact, one of the
most noticeable characteristics of the play. The contrivance achieves its most effective use in the scene
where large crowds emit meaningless sounds, as in the
interrogative "kasrigogh, kasrigogh?" [3.4].

As occurred in serious baroque drama, the action is
complicated by a puntiglio, or point of honor, which
stymies the mission of the ambassadors. The Athenians

are not inclined to follow the Persian ritual of adora-
tion of Alexander. The problem could be solved by having
the king wear an effigy of Pallas Athena on his helmet,
so that the ambassadors would actually be prostrating
themselves not before the monarch, but before a goddess.
But the grotesque situation, which not even the presence
of Aristotle can resolve, is exacerbated when pranksters
substitute Pallas's image with an owl. The ensuing
scenes of pandemonium are reminiscent of Dante's technique of incorporating "comic" elements in the Malebolge
scenes of his Inferno; namely, his underscoring of the
action—as Alfieri well knew—by the use of jarring realistic language and harsh-sounding verses. Alfieri's
cynicism seems to have reached such a degree that he
could see in humanity only its inability to communicate
within any given social structure. The basic message
conveyed by the chaotic action of I Troppi is that any
hope for social agreement would have to reside outside of
the boundaries of reality. Hence the fantastic setting
of the following play, L'Antidoto.

The last comedy of the tetralogy departs from familiar
historical scenes, transporting the reader to an imaginary island in the Orcades Archipelagus—to the home of
Pigliatutto (Grab-everything), king of the island, and
Pigliapoco (Grab-little), his brother-in-law. The utopian rather than exotic setting is interwoven with an
allegorical apparatus whose meaning is transparently
clear. A shipwrecked magician prophesies that Pigliatutto's wife, Piglianchella (She-grabs-too), will give
birth to a protean monster who can assume three shapes:
without legs (symbolizing monarchy); three-headed, but
with no hands (oligarchy); or without a head (democracy).
The ghosts of Darius, Caius Graccus, and Demosthenes
appear, personifying the three institutional types portrayed in the previous plays; Darius even advises to opt
for monarchy. But an amazingly beautiful girl, born
amidst thundering earthquakes, and growing rapidly into
her twenties, establishes a new political structure which
harmoniously blends the contribution of each of the
diverse social groups.

The planned title of the comedy was La Magna Carta
Personificata (The Magna Carta personified), where the
allusion to the British type of constitutional government
was more than apparent (32). The meaning and significance of L'Antidoto points to the terminal point of the
tetralogy. Alfieri's political dreams, his libertarian

ideals, when ultimately confronted with reality could
only result in a compromise, but a constructive compromise; the negative posture could perhaps be left behind.
No more heroics punctuated by dramatic and drastic ges-
tures. What we have here is a sedate recourse to the
example of a widely admired political establishment
already tested by time. That the end result should be
positive was implied in the poetics of "usefulness":
Alfieri had faithfully followed its inherent morality
during his entire writing career.

The Heart of Man

La finestrina (The little window) and Il Divorzio
(Divorce) are, in that order, Alfieri's last two works.
In the latter the poet has chosen, surprisingly enough,
to place the play's action against a contemporary Italian
backdrop: the setting chosen is the city of Genoa. Paradoxically, in the last phase of his life, in the moment
that saw him withdrawing more and more into the choice
company of Greek and Latin authors, Alfieri directly
confronts the social reality of his own country in his
own time. His critical stance is apparent from the title
Il Divorzio, for, ironically, the play does not deal
with a divorce, but with a wedding.
Lucrezia, the young daughter of Annetta and Agostino
Gherdolosi, rather than marrying Prosperino, an honest
and—as the name indicates—wealthy young man, marries
the old and ugly Stomaconi. She does this in order to
assure for herself the maximum degree of independence;
the freedom to choose as many cicisbei ("gallant es-
corts") as she pleases. Her first choice is Ciuffini,
her mother's favorite; Lucrezia is ready to offer, in
exchange, her own husband! The deleterious aspects of
cicisbeismo had been prominent in the elegant, satiric
poem by Giuseppe Parini (1729-1799) Il Giorno (The
Day—a day in the life of an idle young nobleman) and
even in the Sermoni (Satires) of Gasparo Gozzi (1713-
1786). On the stage, Goldoni had provided the public
with a wide variety of social types, with all their idio-
syncracies and changing moods determined either by age,
social position, or economic state. While recapitulating
most of these elements, Alfieri's Il Divorzio is more
scathing than Goldoni's theater in the scrutiny of individual characters, more biting than Parini's rather

nostalgic depiction of aristocracy, and more melancholy
even than the moody Gozzi. All of the author's indignation explodes in the end in Agostino's invective: "Oh
fetor dei costumi Italianeschi" (Oh stench of the Italian
way of life!). Alas, says the poet, there is no need of
divorce in Italy, for every matrimonial union is, in
fact, a disunion.

Alfieri insisted that he would rather have people
laugh than feel ashamed, but in essence Il Divorzio is
a strong moral indictment, and the laughter can only be
sardonic. He had chosen such a theme for his only "modern" play in a significant attempt to correct society in
his "vile century"; he intended to place in sharp focus a
pernicious social disease affecting its basic cell, the
family. That this was done in a comic vein did not dimin-
ish the seriousness of the intent; it merely made the
play somewhat more palatable.

La finestrina, on the other hand, expresses the ultimate in Alfieri's pessimistic outlook on life. Breaking
away from any particular, limiting, sociopolitical structure, the poet addresses himself to a universal question:
the fundamental value and essence of human nature.

Conceived and written before Il Divorzio, this play
was, nonetheless, the last labor of Alfieri; his tireless
ripulitura ("polishing") and elaboration were interrupted a few days before his death, at the eighth scene
of the third act (33). The setting, possibly inspired by
Aristophanes' Frogs, is the Underworld, where Mercury
has been sent by Jupiter to investigate the three infer-
nal judges: Minos, Aeacus, and Rhadamanthus. Apparently, they have been allowing entrance to the Elysian
Fields to souls not entirely worthy of that privilege.
Still faithful to his aristocratic bent and to Aristotle's Poetics, Alfieri's examples of those false
pretenders include only high-caliber achievers, in both
good and evil. Only their deeds, however, have so far
been judged, not their intentions. Since Rhadamanthus is
rather lethargic and always follows Aeacus's opinions, it
is the latter's liberal justice that constantly prevails.
Aeacus is to be regarded as Alfieri's mouthpiece. The
eighteenth-century brand of morality that operates in
this comedy is in fact based upon the degree of "utility"
to society as displayed by certain individuals.

Mercury has been ordered to open a "little window" in
the hearts of some of the souls who have gained unde-
served access to the Elysian Fields—thus disclosing

their secret motivations. The noblest actions of men, men like Homer, Licurgus, Confucius, and the Prophet Mohammed, were, we discover, spurred by egotistical incentives. In the end, even Mercury himself is not left untarnished by suspicion. There is an uprising in the Elysian Fields and a proposal is made to open a "little window" in the heart of Jupiter's messenger as well, but Mercury, for fear of public humiliation, agrees to put an end to his investigations. Besides, Aeacus has convinced him that great talent is required in judging man, for "Every truth is no truth; and a great part of what appears to be actually is; and unfortunately that which must, should, or could be, is most of the time but a dream" [5.5]. If man is to have peace of mind, he must learn to accept appearance over reality!

After a lifetime of intense scrutiny of mankind, this seems to be a rather cynical conclusion, yet it also seems to reveal a new wisdom which makes it possible to understand better, and accept, humanity as it really is, with all its limitations, over which it is perhaps better to laugh than to weep. But the author's wry smile could be turned even on himself. A few months before his death he wrote to a friend to announce that he had invented a facetious "Knighthood of Homer" and, as a reward for his arduous conquest of classical Greek, he planned to style himself a knight of that order. The member would be inducted by receiving a collar or chain inscribed with the names of the twenty-three greatest poets, ancient and modern. A pendant cameo would have Homer's portrait on one side and, on the back, a Greek distich composed by Alfieri, which stressed the fact that someone had at last come up with a true order of knighthood—that of the spirit. Alfieri was, as we have seen from his poetical attitudes, in many respects an unregenerate aristocrat, yet he could still smile at aristocratic pretensions, including his own (34). This final incident, related by the author in his autobiography, confirms the sense of self-irony that we detected earlier. If we keep in mind the fact that he never, even at the end, lost his ability to laugh at himself, it clarifies and softens the vision of the world he had expressed in his comic theater in general, and in the La finestrina in particular.

When Alfieri died on October 8, 1803, still working on his comedies, he had come full circle: his tragic theater had been given a complementary comic face. His poetic experience could be emblematically visualized as

composed of the two classical masks of laughter and
sorrow. He had contemplated all the feelings and emotions derived from them in unforgettable characters and
situations. Alfieri's Italy had acquired a theater
worthy of its unique cultural heritage.

Notes and References

Chapter One

1. Ettore Passerin d'Entrèves, "L'Italia nell'età delle riforme; il regno di Sardegna," in Storia d'Italia, ed. Nino Valeri (Turin, 1965), 3:45-74.
2. Ibid., p. 46.
3. Ibid., pp. 48-49.
4. Vita, a cura di Luigi Fassò (Asti, 1951), 1:294-96.
5. Vita, a cura di Luigi Fassò, Prima redazione inedita della Vita, Giornali, Annali e documenti autobiografici, 2:121-23 (vol. 2 of the Opere). Concerning the events related in the Vita up to the year 1790, we have chosen to rely on the first draft, convinced that it preserves the immediacy of their occurrence better than the subsequent corrected version.
6. Ibid., p. 118. Also: "Lettera a Ranieri De' Calzabigi" in Parere sulle tragedie e altre prose critiche, a cura di Morena Pagliai, in Opere (Asti, 1978), pp. 217-18 (vol. 35 of the Opere).
7. Vittore Branca, Alfieri e la ricerca dello stile (Florence, 1959), pp. 227-35.
8. Carmine Jannaco, Studi alfieriani vecchi e nuovi (Florence: Leo S. Olscki, 1974), p. 135. Jannaco's concern—which follows a suggestion made by Fubini—is centered here around the formation of Alfieri's style; the idea of a possible rivalry the poet felt toward Metastasio is ours.
9. Cf. Saverio Bettinelli, Lettere virgiliane e inglesi, a cura di Vittorio Enzo Alfieri (Bari: Laterza, 1930), and Franco Betti, Storia critica delle lettere virgiliane (Verona: Fiorini, 1972).
10. Vita, 2:148-52. Also: Del Principe e delle Lettere, in Scritti morali e politici, I a cura di Pietro Cazzani, in Opere (Asti, 1951) (vol. 3 of the Opere). Here the poet is given a privileged position with respect to his "utility" to society. But cf. especially La virtù sconosciuta, in the same volume, p. 279.

11. Vita, 2:118-19.
12. Ibid., 2:157-59. Cf. also La tragedia classica,
a cura di Giammaria Gasparini, ed. Mario Fubini, vol. 56
(Turin: U.T.E.T., 1963), pp. 19-28. In I classici
italiani, vol. 56.
13. Benedetto Croce, Poesia e non poesia (Bari,
1950), p. 2.
14. Carmine Jannaco, in Vittorio Alfieri, Tragedie,
1:xxxii ff. (vol. 6 of the Opere). Also: Tragedies,
ed. Edgar Alfred Bowring, C.B. (Westport, Conn., 1970),
p. 3. This English version of Alfieri's Tragedies is
derived, with numerous revisions, from that of Charles
Lloyd (London, 1815). All subsequent English quotations
are from this version. Numbers enclosed in brackets following quotations in the text refer to act and scene:
[5.2] refers to act 5, scene 2.
15. The Prince and Letters (Toronto, 1972), trans.
Beatrice Corrigan and Julius Molinaro, p. 27. Also:
Del Principe e delle Lettere, 1:131.
16. Parere, 35:144-50.
17. Ibid., "Risposta dell'Alfieri," pp. 220-21.
18. Ibid., "Lettera di Ranieri De' Calzabigi," p. 181.
19. Cf. Betti, Storia critica, especially Chap. 2.
20. Parere, 35:157-66.
21. Prince and Letters, Introduction.
22. Ibid., p. 13.
23. Ibid., p. 106.
24. Ibid., p. 153.
25. Ibid., p. 8.
26. Della Tirannide in Scritti morali e politici,
1:17.
27. Elizabeth Ellet, Poems translated and original.
By Mrs. E. F. Ellet (Philadelphia: Key & Biddle, 1835),
p. 35.

Chapter Two

1. Parere, 35:85-86. An interesting way for the
author to defuse possible negative criticism.
2. Ibid., p. 87.
3. Tragedies, 1:52.
4. Jannaco, Introduction to Polinice, in Tragedie
(Asti, 1953), 2:4-5 (vol. 5 of the Opere).
5. Vitilio Masiello, L'ideologia tragica di Vittorio
Alfieri (Rome, 1964), p. 62. On the same note, see also: Riccardo Scrivano, La natura teatrale dell'ispira-

zione alfieriana (Milan-Messina, 1963), p. 70.

6. Antigone, the first of Alfieri's tragedies with only four characters, was conceived in Pisa in June, 1776, together with the Agamennone and Oreste, versified in Turin in 1777, and completed (rifatta) in Rome in 1781. For this chronology, see: Jannaco, Introduction to Antigone in Tragedie (Asti, 1953), 3:3-7 (vol. 8 of the Opere).

7. Parere, pp. 90-93.

8. The tragedy of Antigone was performed in Rome, on November 20, 1782, in the private theater of the Spanish Ambassador, with the author playing the role of Creon. Cf. Alfieri, Vita, pp. 181-82. Also: Tragedies, 1:102.

9. Vita, p. 260. Also: Jannaco and Raffaele De Bello, in Tragedie (Asti, 1967), 5:3 (vol. 16 of the Opere).

10. Vita, p. 151.

11. Parere, pp. 97-102.

12. Ibid., p. 99.

13. Ibid., p. 101.

14. Oreste, a cura di Raffaele De Bello, in Tragedie (Asti, 1967), 6:142 where Alfieri's first draft of Oreste is reproduced (vol. 17 of the Opere).

Chapter Three

1. Virginia, a cura di C. Jannaco, in Tragedie (Asti, 1955), 4:14 (vol. 13 of the Opere).

2. Scrivano, Natura teatrale, p. 65. Scrivano points to the rhetorical aspects of the "tragedies of liberty" but he also recognizes the poetic afflatus attained by Alfieri in the Congiura.

3. "Lettera dell'abate Cesarotti" and "Note dell' Alfieri che servono di risposta," in Parere, pp. 249-77; esp. p. 118 where the author gives us his opinion on Timoleone in reference to Virginia and the Congiura.

4. Ibid., p. 94.

5. Tragedies 1:152-53. See also Pino Mensi, Gli affetti nella tragedia di Vittorio Alfieri (Padova: Cedam, 1974), pp. 79-86. Also: Raffaello Ramat, Vittorio Alfieri (Florence: Sandron, 1964), p. 235. Ramat has interesting comments on the illustrations that adorned the Ciardetti edition of Alfieri's tragedies (Firenze, 1820), reflecting the patriotic criticism of the time. The iconography tended toward a melodramatic

and operatic interpretation and popularization of
Alfieri's theater.

6. Parere, p. 118.
7. "Risposta al Cesarotti," pp. 265-67.
8. Tragedies 1:419.
9. Ibid.
10. Ibid., p. 421.
11. Parere, p. 264.
12. Don Garzia, a cura di Lovanio Rossi, in Tragedie (Asti, 1975), 13:11 (vol. 26 of the Opere).
13. Vita, p. 237. Also: Walter Binni, Saggi
Alfieriani (Florence, 1969), p. 41.
14. Parere, p. 105.
15. Cf. Aristotle's Poetics, with an introductory
essay by Francis Fergusson (New York: Hill & Wang,
1965), pp. 78-80. Also: Masiello, Ideologia tragica,
p. 113.
16. Parere, p. 105.
17. Ibid., pp. 111-12.
18. Ibid., p. 115.
19. Maria Stuarda, a cura di Raffaele De Bello, in
Tragedie (Asti, 1970), 11:3-9 (vol. 18 of the Opere).
20. Tragedies 1:528. Also: De Bello's Introduction
to Maria Stuarda, 11:8. About the same incident cf.
Vita, Chapters 7, 8, 18.
21. Parere, p. 115.
22. Ibid.
23. Aristotle's Poetics, pp. 11, 18.
24. Cf. "Lettera dell'abate Cesarotti," in Parere,
pp. 250-52.
25. "Risposta," in Parere, p. 145.
26. Vita, p. 145.
27. Ibid., p. 178.
28. Scipione Maffei, Merope, in Tragedia Classica,
p. 670.

Chapter Four

1. Vita, p. 178. By that time Alfieri felt that he
had reached his goal of writing no more than twelve tragedies, but eventually he changed his mind and went on to
write seven more.
2. Parere, p. 121.
3. Concerning the protoromanticismo of Alfieri, see
Benedetto Croce, Poesia e non poesia, p. 2.
4. The "faithful" Michal is a purely Alfierian crea-

tion; in the biblical version she is not depicted as so virtuous.

5. For a penetrating discussion of Saul's "old age" see Binni, "Lettura del Saul," in Saggi alfieriani, pp. 71-118.

6. Parere, p. 122.

7. Binni, Lettura, p. 99 n. Of great interest are Binni's observations concerning the language of Saul which he sees as the result of a fruitful encounter between the Bible and the "Ossianic" poetry which had been made fashionable at the time in Italy by Cesarotti; cf. p. 75.

8. David's singing is one of the weak points of the tragedy and Alfieri himself had his share of doubts; see Parere, p. 123. Since it reflects the various genres of lyrical poetry of the Italian eighteenth century, however, it has great cultural interest. In this regard cf. again Binni, "Lettura del Saul," p. 105.

9. Saul's tirade against the priests is also of a certain significance especially in view of the evolution of the author's satirical vein.

10. This exemplary Catonian form of suicide greatly impressed the young Foscolo who then produced his own version, personified by Jacopo Ortis in his epistolary novel which bears his name.

11. Vita, p. 178.

12. Ibid., p. 180.

13. Epistolario, I a cura di Lanfranco Caretti (Asti, 1963), p. 190 (vol. 14 of the Opere).

14. Parere, p. 124.

15. Tragedies, 2:124.

16. Parere, p. 125.

17. Ibid., pp. 130-31.

Chapter Five

1. Scritti morali e politici, 1:x ff. Also Vita, pp. 202-17. Del Principe e delle Lettere (The Prince and Letters), 1786; the Dialogo della Virtù sconosciuta (The dialogue on unrecognized virtue), 1786; Della Tirannide (On Tyranny), 1787; the Panegirico di Plinio a Traiano (Panegyric of Pliny to Trajan), 1787; the tragedies Bruto Primo (The First Brutus), 1787, and Bruto Secondo (The Second Brutus), 1786-88; and the Parere sulle Tragedie (Opinion on his tragedies), 1789. All the while he was versifying and correcting

several tragedies, polishing the Rime (Poems), writing
his first satirical composition and a favoletta, or
fable. The outcome of all this activity was the complete
edition of the tragedies (Paris: Didot, 1787–89), and of
his other works (Kehl: Beaumarchais, 1790).

2. Vita, pp. 230–50.
3. Scritti politici e morali, 1:5.
4. Ibid., p. 115.
5. Ibid., "Dialogo," pp. 261–62.
6. The Prince and Letters, p. 57.
7. Ibid., p. 97.
8. Ibid., p. 292.
9. Parere, pp. 134–43.
10. Rime, a cura di Francesco Maggini (Asti, 1954),
p. xv (vol. 9 of the Opere). For the development of
Alfieri's lyrical style, see especially, Branca, Alfieri
e la ricerca dello stile, pp. 3–124. Also: Binni, Saggi alfieriani, Chap. 5 and Appendice; Chaps. 3, 4.
Still of some interest is the laborious work by Maria
Cappuccio, Le rime di Vittorio Alfieri (Capua: Solari,
1932).
11. Rime, p. ix. Also: Vita, p. 120.
12. Rime, p. xxi.
13. Vita, pp. 251–55. See also Fassò's Introduction to the same volume.
14. Aristotle's Poetics, p. 82.
15. Vita, p. 231.
16. Ibid., p. 250, translation mine.
17. Ibid., pp. 54–55.
18. Ibid., p. 27. This important statement was retained by the author in the later revised version.
19. Ibid., p. 71.
20. Ibid., p. 64, translation mine.

Chapter Six

1. Vita, 1:294.
2. Epistolario, a cura di Lanfranco Caretti (Asti,
1963), 1:339 (vol. 14 of Opere). The author also added
that he intended to spend the rest of his life—after the
forty-sixth year—in silence, refining his works and publishing them.
3. Vita, 1:286. On Alfieri's concern for style,
see Branca, Alfieri e la ricerca dello stile, p. 160
ff.
4. Masiello, Ideologia tragica, p. 275.

5. Misogallo, in Opere (Florence, 1806), vol. 17. There is no modern critical edition of this work.

6. Ibid., p. 11 n.

7. Ibid., p. 18.

8. Satire, in Opere (Florence, 1806), 6:3. There is no modern critical edition of this work.

9. Ibid., p. 15.

10. Ibid., p. 18.

11. Ibid., pp. 25-29.

12. Masiello, Ideologia tragica, p. 285.

13. Satire, 6:31.

14. Masiello, Ideologia tragica, p. 287.

15. Satire, p. 92.

16. Masiello, Ideologia tragica, p. 289.

17. Satire, p. 38.

18. Ibid., pp. 94-95 ff.

19. Masiello, Ideologia tragica, p. 291.

20. Vita, 1:291.

21. Ibid., p. 345.

22. Ibid., 2:294. It has been conjectured that this notice was put on by Alfieri during the second French occupation of Florence in 1800.

23. Ibid., 1:339 ff.

24. Fiorenzo Forti, Introduction to Alfieri, Commedie (Asti, 1953), 1:xii (vol. 10 of the Opere). From Forti's accurate reconstruction of the events, we learn that on September 14, 1799, Alfieri conceived four of the comedies; the other two on September 16 of the same year. In the same Introduction, Forti draws attention to the "Terzi pensieri comici" of 1790, where the author ironically states that after courting sloth, glory, and nothingness, he finally "married" comedy.

25. Vita, 1:342. Also Carla Doni, Vittorio Alfieri traduttore dei classici latini (Padua: Liviana, 1980). Also Branca, Alfieri e la ricerca dello stile, pp. 159-84, where particular attention is given to Alfieri as translator of Pope's Essay on Criticism. See especially p. 181 n.

26. Giuseppe Santarelli, Studi e ricerche sulla genesi e le fonti delle commedie alfieriane (Milan: Bietti, 1971), p. 27 ff.

27. Ibid., p. 35.

28. Ibid., pp. 37, 51, 52.

29. Commedie, p. 207. Also Vincenzo Placella, Alfieri comico (Bergamo-Milan-Florence-Rome-Bari-Messina, 1973), p. 202.

30. Ibid., p. 208.
31. Commedie, 2:235 n.
32. Ibid., 1:211.
33. Ibid., p. xxiii.
34. Vita, 1:349–51.

Selected Bibliography

PRIMARY SOURCES

The best available edition of Alfieri's works is the
critical edition of the Opere di Vittorio Alfieri da
Asti, Casa d'Alfieri, begun in 1951, promoted by the
city and province of Asti, and entrusted to the care of
the Centro Nazionale Di Studi Alfieriani. While the work
is still in the process of completion, we already have
thirty-six volumes (the most recent one published in
1978), containing all of Alfieri's major works: the Tragedie, Commedie, Vita, Rime, Scritti Morali e
Politici, and the poet's correspondence or Epistolario. Each work is edited by a renowned scholar, or
team of scholars, and, in addition to the text of the
critical edition, contains all the various drafts in
their original versions. A vast network of biographical
and bibliographical references makes each volume an indispensable working tool.

1. Other editions
Opere. Florence: Piatti, 1807. 20 vols. An elegant
    and rare edition, containing most of Alfieri's
    writings with the exception of the Epistolario.
Opere. Pisa: Capurro, 1805–1815. 22 vols. A rare
    edition of only 250 copies.
Opere. Naples: Rossi-Romano, 1861. 14 vols.
Opere. Turin: Paravia, 1903. 11 vols. Printed for
    the centennial of the author's death. Guido Bustico,
    Bibliografia di Vittorio Alfieri. Florence:
    Olschki, 1927, lists, in 258 pages, all of the com-
    plete, partial, and single-work editions of Alfieri's
    writings from the author's time up to 1927.

2. Translations
Translations of Alfieri's works are so numerous—
particulary into French—that we must refer the reader to
the above-mentioned bibliography compiled by Bustico.
However, the list of English translations that are both

reliable and available is very short.

The Autobiography of Vittorio Alfieri. Translated,
with an original essay on the genius and times of
Alfieri, by C. Edwards Lester. New York: Paine &
Burgess, 1845. This translation, the first in the
U.S., was successful enough to see another printing in
the same year.

Life of Vittorio Alfieri. Boston: J. R. Osgood, 1877.
With an essay by William D. Howells. As Howells
explains (p. 51), this is a reprint of an anonymous
version of Alfieri's Vita published in London in
1810. The essay which precedes the translation contains excerpts from the Agamennone and the Oreste,
and two sonnets, one of which is the famous self-
portrait "Thou mirror of veracious speech sublime."
The same book was later reprinted in Boston in 1883
and 1905.

The Life of Vittorio Alfieri written by himself. Translated by Sir Henry Mc Anally. Lawrence: University
of Kansas Press, 1953.

Memoirs. Anonymous translation of 1810, revised by E.
R. Vincent. London & New York: Oxford University
Press, 1961.

Of Tyranny. Translated, edited and with an introduction by Julius A. Molinaro and Beatrice Corrigan.
Toronto: University of Toronto Press, 1961.

The Prince and Letters. Translated by Beatrice
Corrigan and Julius A. Molinaro, with introduction and
notes by B. Corrigan. Toronto: University of Toronto
Press, 1972.

Three Comedies by Carlo Goldoni, Three Tragedies by
Vittorio Alfieri. New York: The National Alumni,
1907. Includes The Conspiracy of the Pazzi, Mary
Stuart, and Antigone, translated by Charles Lloyd.

The Tragedies of Vittorio Alfieri, complete, including
his posthumous works. Westport, Conn.: Greenwood
Press, 1970. A reprint of the volume, based on
Charles Lloyd's translation, edited by Edgar Alfred
Bowring, who also translated the posthumously pub-
lished plays (London: G. Bell & Sons, 1876).

SECONDARY SOURCES

Bertana, Emilio. Vittorio Alfieri. Turin: Loescher,
1902. An exemplary work of the positivistic era of
literary criticism, it fails to identify the Romantic

tension of Alfieri's poetical world. It does, however, point out the complexity of the author's character and also furnishes the expert reader with abundant
and valuable data.

Binni, Walter. <u>Saggi Alfieriani</u>. Florence: La Nuova
Italia, 1969. Contains numerous essays previously
published by Binni throughout his career. The best of
them, such as the essay on Alfieri's <u>Letters</u> and the
<u>Rime</u>, or those on <u>Saul</u> and <u>Mirra</u>, illuminate the
"human" dimension of Alfieri's works and emphasize
the ties of his theater with the preceding Italian
tradition.

Bosco, Umberto. <u>Lirica alfieriana</u>. Asti: Casa
d'Alfieri, 1943. Recognizes the validity of Alfieri's
lyrical production in its own right.

Branca, Vittore. <u>Alfieri e la ricerca dello stile</u>.
Florence: Le Monnier, 1948. A major contribution to
the study of the evolution of Alfieri's hard-conquered
poetic style.

Calcaterra, Carlo. <u>Il barocco in Arcadia</u>. Bologna:
Zanichelli, 1950. Contains two essays which illus-
trate with great erudition, the relationship between
Alfieri's <u>Polinice</u> and <u>Antigone</u> and the works of
Statius.

Calosso, Umberto. <u>L'anarchia di Vittorio Alfieri</u>.
Bari: G. Laterza, 1949. A stimulating study which
takes to its extreme limits Croce's thesis of
Alfieri's individualism. The poet's work is seen as
the expression of an anarchic will to power.

Ceccoli, Ines. <u>L'eroina alfieriana</u>. Bologna: L.
Cappelli, 1926. One of the first works dealing with
the feminine characters in Alfieri's theater.

Croce, Benedetto. <u>Poesia e non Poesia</u>. Bari: Laterza, 1950. Contains pages on Alfieri that Croce had
already published in his review "Critica," in 1917. A
turning point in Alfieri criticism, it underscores the
poet's "Proto-Romanticism" on the one hand, and the
complexity of the single character as the true tragic
nucleus of his theater on the other.

De Sanctis, Francesco. <u>Teoria e storia della lettera-</u>
<u>tura</u>. Edited by B. Croce. Bari: Laterza, 1926. A
revealing judgment passed in the light of the patriotic brand of criticism typical of the nineteenth-
century Italian Risorgimento. Alfieri the man emerges
greater than Alfieri the poet. The intuitive effort
made by the great critic De Sanctis to grasp the total

meaning of Alfieri's poetic achievement remains nonetheless one of the most intense assessments prior to
the twentieth century.

Ferrero, Giuseppe. L'anima e la poesia di Vittorio
Alfieri. Turin: Paravia, 1932. An amplification of
Calosso's theory on Alfieri's idividualism.

Fubini, Mario. Vittorio Alfieri, il pensiero; la tragedia. Florence: Sansoni, 1937. Though centering
again on Alfieri's individualism, Fubini's discussion
goes beyond it by isolating its component of pessimism, regarded, however, not in a personal dimension,
but as an expression of human frailty in general. One
of the fundamental studies on Alfieri.

Fubini, Mario. Ritratto dell'Alfieri e altri studi
alfieriani. Florence: La Nuova Italia, 1951. An
elaboration and amplification of the preceding work.

Maier, Bruno. Alfieri. Palermo: Palumbo, 1962. A
most valuable anthology of Alfieri criticism from the
poet's time up to 1949.

Masiello, Vitilio. L'ideologia tragica di Vittorio
Alfieri. Rome: Edizioni Dell'Ateneo, 1964. In his
brilliant and well-documented discussion Masiello
makes of Alfieri the last exponent of Humanism; his
work is regarded as the expression of the crisis of
the Enlightenment at the dawning of a new era.

Momigliano, Attilio. Vittorio Alfieri, Saul, interpre-
tato da A. Momigliano con un saggio introduttivo.
Catania: Muglia, 1921. Vittorio Alfieri, Mirra,
interpretata da A. Momigliano, con un saggio introduttivo. Florence: Vallecchi, 1923. These are possibly
the best close readings, from an aesthetic point of
view, of these two works. Alfieri's individualism
takes on a new complexion: the heroes of the tragedies are regarded not as the celebration of an individualistic thirst for power, but rather as the
expression of a moral drama determined by the wish of
the individual to preserve the purity and freedom of
his soul in the face of an hostile world.

Placella, Vincenzo. Alfieri comico. Milan-Florence-
Rome-Bari-Messina: Minerva Italica, 1973. A detailed
and well-documented essay essential to the study of
Alfieri's comic theater and its classical sources.

Porena, Manfredi. Vittorio Alfieri e la tragedia.
Milan: Hoepli, 1904. A vast, rather antiquated work,
whose value lies mainly in the comparative discussion
of Alfieri's theater and its classical antecedents.

Ramat, Raffaello. <u>Vittorio Alfieri, saggi.</u> Florence: Sandron, 1964. A lyrical reading of Alfieri's tragedies.

Russo, Luigi. <u>Ritratti e disegni storici.</u> Serie prima. Bari: Laterza, 1946. Russo too proposes a lyrical interpretation of Alfieri's theater.

Santarelli, Giuseppe. <u>Studi e ricerche sulla genesi e le fonti delle commedie alfieriane.</u> Milan: Bietti, 1971. A philologically sound analysis of the classical sources of inspiration for Alfieri's comedies.

Scrivano, Riccardo. <u>La natura teatrale dell'ispirazione alfieriana.</u> Milan-Messina: Principato, 1963. Following the path of Fubini and Binni, Scrivano has gathered in this volume several essays on different aspects of Alfieri's work. A stimulating and exhaustive portrait of the tragic poet.

Trovato, Mario. <u>Il messaggio poetico dell'Alfieri: la natura del limite tragico.</u> Rome: Edizioni dell' Ateneo & Bizzarri, 1978. A penetrating study on the source and nature of Alfieri's poetical inspiration and tragic representation.

Index